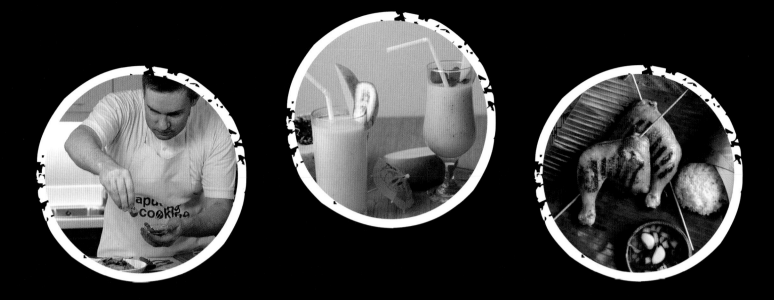

# THE WORLD OF FILIPINO COOKING

## Food and Fun in the Philippines

### By Chris Urbano
#### of *"Maputing Cooking"*

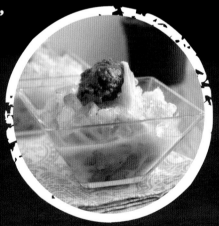

# CONTENTS

# Filipino Food Goes Global

Much has been written on the imminent arrival of Filipino food on the world stage—it's a cuisine that has not so far enjoyed the global fame and adoption of others, despite a growing awareness and advocacy around the world through one of the world's largest and most active diasporas. And until now, it remains largely off the radar of foodies around the world. It has been said that Filipino food is misunderstood, that it is bland, lacking complexity or repulsive for weird ingredients and "frankenfoods": like duck embryos, coagulated pig's blood or chicken intestines on a stick. But having traveled and dined widely across Southeast Asia, I've discovered that while certainly misunderstood, this is a cuisine that is well ahead of the times. Through twists of history the Filipino cuisine has been influenced by almost every major global culinary tradition, and has remarkably integrated and innovated on these and made them its own—and yes, its time is coming.

Growing up in suburban Australia, the idea of going to a Filipino restaurant or takeout was—even till today—not common. So it has been to my great surprise to find myself now living in Manila as a chef specializing in Filipino culinary arts; and one of the pioneers of a global "Filipino Food Movement" that is underway, through my online cooking program and blog *Maputing Cooking* (literally meaning "a white foreigner cooking").

Filipinos often leave comments on my videos that they feel so proud to see a foreigner truly knowing and appreciating their food, many are in fact surprised that a foreigner can be so in love with their cuisine, or believes their cuisine to be world class. Just as the grass appears greener on the other side of the fence, for Filipinos growing up eating this cuisine daily, it's easy to underestimate the culinary value it represents. *Maputing Cooking* has proven popular through portraying the food in a new light, through fresh eyes experiencing Filipino food for the first time. This book is an account of my discovery and interpretations of Filipino food—told through the eyes of a *foreign-noy*, or "foreigner with the heart of a Filipino".

Food and culture go hand in hand. When I first arrived in Manila over a decade ago to study *wikang Filipino* (Filipino language), Philippine history and politics I found that it was through sharing a meal with the Filipinos that I got the clearest insight into the Filipino culture and society. As a passionate home chef and foodie myself, food and cooking was a perfect reason to explore the Philippines, connect with the people, and learn the language. I spent my time in the traditional wet markets of Quezon or Mandaluyong cities, chatting with the market vendors who are only too happy to chat with a foreigner who's so fascinated with their food. Indeed it was from these conversations that I picked up my first Filipino recipes, and I would practice cooking them at home after buying my ingredients from these same people.

As time went by and my knowledge of the language and history of the Philippines increased, I started to see the imprint of historical events on Filipino food and how it took shape over the centuries. From the Austronesian migration across the region to the spread of religion, culture and trade from China, India and the Malay peninsula; from the Spanish colonial period, to the American administration in the 20th century: the fingerprints of history are found everywhere in Filipino food.

The very reason Filipino food can be hard to understand, or is known for powerful and sometimes "strange" food juxtapositions is that it is the product of an equally complex history, and myriad of cultural influences. In today's culinary landscape, "fusion" is a word used to describe a multicultural combination of dishes from different parts of the world. It's East Asian meets Southeast Asian, or Asian meets Western cuisine, a clash of tastes and cultures. It's the future of food. But in the Philippines, this "fusion" happened gradually over the past centuries, forming a melting pot of indigenous, Malay, Chinese, Spanish and

**Left and below:** Filipino food uses a wide range of cooking techniques, and comes in an equally wide range of forms.

**Above and right:** Fried chicken was popularized only after the Americans introduced deep frying; while Chicken Sotanghon is colored with annatto seeds brought by the Mexico Galleon trade.

American cooking. And this is probably the best way to describe what Filipino food is today. Most Filipino recipes today are inherently "fusion" with two or more culinary traditions clearly evident. Through the vicissitudes and accidents of history, Filipino food may well be known as the first true global fusion cuisine—ahead of its time indeed.

And this was how I became hooked—every dish a fascinating insight into the past. This is the country that matches Spanish *leche flan* with tropical yams; Mexican chocolate rice with dried fish; Chinese black beans with pineapples; Malay style coconut curries with taro leaves; American hotdogs with spaghetti. While some dishes appear truly unusual, Filipino chefs have created harmonies between the taste sensations of sweet, salty, sour, bitter and savory with remarkable consistency. For example in the Filipino Nilagang Baka or boiled beef soup, one will find a remarkably diverse set of ingredients: beef, banana, native limes and fish sauce in a single perfectly balanced meal.

After a fascinating year of discovery in my college days I returned to Australia to complete my studies and started a career in business. But my passion for Filipino food and cooking never faded and in 2014 I returned to Manila on a permanent basis to start my own business in the food and beverage industry. And due to my passion for the cuisine, I set a goal to help culinary arts both locally and internationally—starting with my *Maputing Cooking* Youtube videos and blog.

With the support and well wishes of Filipinos worldwide, I've been privileged to present Filipino food to a global audience directly through the show, local and international media appearances, as a representative for food and culinary brands in the Philippines, and as a culinary ambassador from the Philippines to countries abroad, including my native country Australia.

As one of the few Tagalog speaking foreigners based in Manila, I'm a proud *foreign-noy* and glad to be a part of the movement that is showcasing this remarkable culinary legacy to the world. Whether you're a Filipino *kababayan*, or a foreigner keen to discover the unique flavors of Filipino cooking, I trust you'll find this book—seen through the eyes of a *foreign-noy*—a complete reference on how Filipino food came to be, where it is going and how to eat, enjoy, prepare and cook this truly global cuisine.

*Kain na tayo*!

# The Remarkable Origins of Filipino Cooking

As an archipelago of 7,107 islands, the Philippines is a hotbed of diversity which has seen numerous invited and uninvited guests step ashore over the centuries, leaving their marks on the culture, food and culinary landscape of the country. Ask any Filipino "What is Filipino food?" and the answer would probably be *adobo, sinigang, kare-kare, kilawin* or *lumpia*. In those five dishes one will find the ingredients and cooking techniques common to major culinary traditions around the world. The truth is, it's all of those—and more. A hodgepodge of recipes from around the world that washed ashore through the archipelago over the centuries have evolved into what might be best described as "Asian fusion soul food, without limits".

With the diverse microclimates of a tropical archipelago, Filipino recipes tend to adjust based on the surrounding nature, the availability of various ingredients and their

**A typical Philippine wet market features an array of fresh and processed foods with origins around the world.**

relative abundance in nearby land or sea. This meant a number of Filipino recipes actually represent a method or genre of cooking, rather than a specific set of ingredients—the recipe varies according to the local region. For instance, *sinigang* is cooked in various ways depending on which region it was cooked, it could include pork, beef, fish or shrimp, and be soured using tamarind, *kamias*, calamansi or unripe guava, papaya or mango. A myriad of vegetables can be used— depending on what's available locally.

Improvisation is the key in Filipino cooking, so it is an ideal cuisine for home chefs who often have to contend with what is available in the fridge or local supermarkets. Perhaps this improvisation mindset is the reason why Filipino chefs so readily experiment with new ingredients and techniques and are so quick to integrate the global culinary influences that have shaped Filipino cuisine over the centuries. The major culinary influences that have shaped Filipino cuisine are the early people migrating to Philippines from Southeast Asia; early trade with China; the Spanish colonial period (including the Mexican Galleon trade) and the American civil administration period. A number of other major world cuisines have played minor roles in the evolution of Filipino cooking, including Indian, Middle Eastern, and more recently, anywhere where a large Overseas Filipino Worker population can be found.

## Island Southeast Asia

Little written record of Filipino cuisine exists prior to the year 1521 when Spanish conquistadors first landed in Mactan, Cebu. However archeological evidence suggests that the archipelago may have been populated by human life as long as 47,000 years ago. The earliest eating habits of prehistoric Filipinos have been traced through carbon dating. Food archaeologist Avelino M. Legazpi excavated dried guava in a bowl in a 14th and 15th century burial in Pangasinan where remains of fish, shellfish and animals were seen. Other excavations have indicated that taro, sweet potato and yam all formed a part of the Filipino prehistoric diet. In Cagayan, pig and chicken bones were found dating back to 2,800 years ago.

The earliest influences on this simple pre-historic fare came via the movement of people, early trade and the associated exchange of language and culture with neighboring countries—particularly the Malay peninsula and Indonesia, which share a number of similar dishes with Philippines. Malaysia's sour soup *singgang* resembles *sinigang*; banana fritters *maruya* is similar to Indonesia's *pisang goreng kipas*; the *kakanin sapin-sapin* is a relative of Thailand's *khanom chan*; and Philippines' *lugaw* is similar to Vietnam's *chao ga*.

Another area of considerable culinary overlap is the way coconut is used in cooking in both the Philippines and its neighboring Southeast Asian countries. Filipino dishes containing coconut are known as *ginataan* (literally to "cook in coconut"). Filipino dishes that use coconut are Laing (page 78) and Bicol style Ginataang Manok (page 99). These recipes share similar flavor profiles with Malay *gulai* or *rendang*.

## Early Trade with China

The Philippines' ties with China were largely via trade and date back to as early as the 10th century. The Philippines is mentioned in early Chinese records where it was referred to as "Ma-Yi" by Chinese traders. While the earliest written evidence of interaction between the two countries was in 982 AD, archeology finds suggest that barter trade had been going on long before this time: trade pottery excavated in Laguna dates back to the Tang Dynasty.

Traders exchange goods such as silk, porcelain, soy products like soy sauce and tofu, seasonings, noodles, sausages, ducks, cook wares, and other foods that became essential parts of the Filipino daily diet. Alongside the arrival of new kitchen utensils like *sianse* and *carajay* (wok), Chinese cooking techniques also crept its way into Filipino homes.

It wasn't long before local adaptations sprung up across the Philippines based on their respective regional produce. Malabon came up with *pancit malabon*, it features oysters, shrimps and squid as toppings; Lucban Quezon has *pancit*

*habhab*, which is eaten off the banana leaf and best paired with vinegar as *sawsawan*; and *marilao*, Bulacan's *pancit* has crumbled rice crisps as toppings. And then there's *pancit luglug*, rice noodles seasoned with shrimp and ground pork sauce, topped with fried garlic, fried tofu, hard boiled egg, *chicharon*, smoked fish, chopped scallions (green onions) and boiled shrimp.

In addition to new recipes, trade with China also brought new ingredients that have been incorporated into existing Filipino cooking. The use of soy products like soy sauce, tofu and *taosi* (fermented black soybeans) is of Chinese influence along with vegetables such as *pechay*, *togue*, and *mustasa*. No more evident is this influence as in Adobo, which most often combines soy sauce with local cane vinegar, which is a major departure from the indigenous *adobong puti* (white adobo) where the meat is cooked in vinegar only. *Taosi* likewise added saltiness to balance sweetness in dishes like the pineapple based pork *humba*.

## The Spanish Colonial Period and Galleon Trade

Over three centuries of colonial occupation, the Spanish influence on Filipino cooking left a lasting mark, introduced of new ingredients and cooking techniques from both Old World and New.

The Spanish brought a diverse mix of sugar, saffron, rice, fruits and vegetables like orange, lemons, and spinach as well as common Mediterranean ingredients including olive oil, eggplants, chickpeas, sweet red peppers and paprika. Many Spanish dishes were meat heavy, favoring pork in particular, while their method of sautéing and stewing, requires olive oil, which was an expensive commodity.

As a result Spanish food was initially consumed only by the social elite, but was slowly disseminated to the wider population through the teachings of housewives, or servant cooks, who worked in the kitchens of Spanish expatriates or *mestizos*. Over time and as living standards rose, dishes like *mechado*, *afritada*, *morcon*, and *embutido* became commonplace in the kitchens of ordinary Filipinos.

With the commencement of the Galleon trade between Manila and Acapulco from 1565 new crop types from the Americas became available. From Mexico came tomatoes, potatoes, cassava, corn, peanuts, bell peppers, chilies, pineapples,

At traditional markets in Manila you'll find vegetables originating from around the world that have entered the cuisine over the centuries.

papaya, guava, sugar apple, custard apple, avocados, jicama, chayote, *cacao*, *guyabano*, *aratiles*, *chico* and *atsuete*. In return, the Philippines traded mangoes, tamarind, rice and tuba.

Spanish-American dishes like *menudo* and *tamales* found their way to the Philippines. Over time Filipinos found ways to incorporate and adapt these to locally available ingredients. In Mexico, *menudo* is a soup comprising beef tripe, tomatoes and peppers, while in the Philippines it has evolved to be a tomato-based stew of chopped pork and liver with potatoes and carrots. *Tamales* is originally a cake made from cornmeal wrapped and cooked in cornhusks while the Filipino version of *tamales* is made from rice, flavored with peanuts, chicken, egg and other condiments steamed in banana leaves.

Cacao became an important commodity as the source of chocolate, which has become a commonplace in Filipino lifestyle. Filipino chefs quickly localized the Mexican chocolate rice porridge *champurrado*, locally known as *champorado*, for cows' milk, and ingeniously serving it with *tuyo* (salty dried fish)—an early precursor to salted chocolate, now popular around the world.

By an accident of geography, the Philippines found itself at the crossroads of the first global colonial empire, where Old World met New World and where the Eastern Hemisphere met the Western. It is unlikely that even the most cosmopolitan European capitals had the same access to such a global diet as could be found in Manila during this time, situated in the heart of the Spice Islands, on the doorstep of China, and a major port for trade goods from both Europe and the Americas.

For over three centuries the Filipino culinary melting pot bubbled away, until the Treaty of Paris in 1898 between the Spanish and US saw the appearance of one last culinary colonizer in the cauldron.

## The American Administrative Period

Between 1902 and 1946, the US enacted sweeping changes that modernized the political administration of the country, and introduced national health and education programs. But the US was also quick to secure long lasting and favorable trade access for US products to the Philippines. This had major implications for the local diet as US industrial food manufacturers flooded the country with canned food, processed meats, tetra packs and modern appliances.

Local kitchens evolved to mimic American kitchens, filled with appliances like freezers ... which replaced traditional clay pots and open wood fires. In home economics classes, young women were taught a more scientific way of cooking and modern hygienic methods. They learned how to cook fried chicken, hot cakes, biscuits, cakes, muffins and other pastries. Their *baon* (lunch) became sandwiches, pastas and salads.

With the advent of television, the local media amplified and accelerated the wave of American influence on Filipino lifestyle and their cuisine. In 1950s, cooking shows were shown in televisions that it was also a chance for manufacturers to promote their products. In the 1960s celebrities like Nora Daza and Virginia Gonzalez popularized industrial foods such as powdered, evaporated and condensed milk and bouillon cubes as substitutes for fresh milk and broths respectively.

The long tradition of women learning how to cook from their mothers and grandmothers in home kitchens was replaced by learning from celebrities. Pre-cooked, pre-mixed, pressure-cooked meals became commonplace in

Filipino homes: hamburgers, fried chicken, steak, pizza, fries, sandwiches and other fast foods were convenient and fast to prepare. Almost overnight a new way of cooking and consuming swept across the Philippines with a focus on convenience, automation and factory made products.

Filipinos adapted these new influences in new and creative ways. Hotdogs were sliced and added to Filipino spaghetti and *pancit*. Sugary sodas were used in improvised street food marinades and for boiling seafood. Apple pies became *buko* (coconut) pies. Ice-cream was flavored with mangos, and cakes with *ube* (purple yam).

Although the US culinary influence has undoubtedly enriched the Filipino cuisine through new ingredients and flavor combinations, the period also led to a decline in the quality of Filipino food and its nutritional value. The US food industry has industrialized its food supply chain to the extent it is now considered bland, and reliant on chemical additives for flavor and preservation. Walking down a Philippines supermarket, it's clear that this trend has rubbed off on Filipino food products too. More saddening is the loss of culinary skill among home cooks, where in many cases, cooking has devolved to a process of combining various canned goods and flavor sachets into something disappointing, flavorless that never lives up to the stylized picture on the packet.

That said, it's truly remarkable to see a cuisine that so nimbly combines American and Asian cooking. My all-time favorite appetizer is Dynamite, a long green chili, stuffed with texmex ground pork filling, American cheddar, wrapped in a *lumpia* wrapper and fried, then served with Ranch dressing. Culinary juxtapositions like this are the defining characteristics of Filipino cuisine today.

## Other Influences on Filipino Cuisine

Indian flavors are certainly evident in a number of Filipino dishes like chicken curry, *kare-kare* and *atchara*. The Indian cultural influence first reached Southeast Asia two millenniums ago through the expansion of the Hindu faith and early barter trade. In more recent centuries, following the brief British occupation of Manila in 1762, groups of Indian soldiers stayed on in the Philippines, and assimilated with the locals. As a livelihood, they started

selling saucy, stew-like dishes they called *kaikaari/kaari* on the streets. Over time, they began to use homegrown ingredients leading to the dish known now as *kare-kare*—now normally served with a side of *bagoong*. Similarly, *atchara* is a close relative of Indian's *achar*, and the name alone suggests a shared culinary origin.

Since the 1990s, other culinary influences have been trickling into the Philippines through the steady stream of Overseas Filipino Workers bringing new flavors home. With hundreds of thousands of Filipinos based in Middle Eastern countries *shawarma* stands are now proliferate in Metro Manila, with new fusion creations resulting from their presence abroad. For example, the *cameleta* (a camel based *caldereta*) is now cooked by Filipinos in the Middle East.

Filipino cuisine continues to evolve to incorporate influences from wherever in the world there are large populations of Filipinos abroad, such as US, Canada, UK, the Middle East, Australia, Japan, Singapore and Hong Kong. Through annual return visits home, or the tradition of sending *balikbayan* boxes laden with food from overseas, new cooking techniques and foods are continually evolving Filipino food which is still very much alive and ever-changing in the 21st century.

**Filipinos enjoy pairing foods with a vast array of *sawsawan*, or dipping sauces, which can introduce a range of eclectic flavors to even simple dishes.**

# Where is Filipino Food Going Now?

As the world becomes increasingly globalized in the 20th and 21st century, so too have specific cuisines evolved around the world—especially so in multi-cultural societies like the US, Canada, UK and Australia. Over the past few decades, we've seen an explosion of Asian cuisines around the world. Chinese food is now ubiquitous around the globe, Japan's sushi, *tonkatsu* or ramen houses are commonplace in cosmopolitan centers of North America and Europe; while other cuisines like Indian, Thai, Vietnamese and Korean have quickly mushroomed after attracting the spotlight of international foodies and critics before being followed by the broader population. Given the vast outbound migration from the Philippines to North America since the 1980s it is somewhat curious then that Filipino food has yet to be pop-ularized as a mainstream cuisine, the way many other Asian cuisines have flourished abroad in recent years.

But first, it's worth considering for a moment what makes a cuisine gain popular global appeal in the first place. Why is it that Chinese, Japanese, Indian or Korean cuisines are now commonplace in the US, whereas Ethiopian, Mongolian, or Burmese cuisine are not? I would suggest that three main factors need to occur for a new cuisine to become popular internationally.

First, it requires a significant and sustained outward migration from a country resulting in the formation of a significant overseas diaspora. Second is that the cuisine must be streamlined and internationalized so it can be understood and enjoyed by people from other cultural back-grounds. And third is the formation of a cadre of passionate chefs, restaurateurs and advocates who have the technical and business skills to both prepare the food at an interna-tional standard and market it to new audiences from differ-ent cultural backgrounds.

People ask me why, with millions of Filipinos having already moved overseas, Filipino food did not take off back in the 80s or 90s? In my view, the reason is that the big wave of Filipino migration largely comprised English speaking and skilled labor, going abroad to take up jobs upon arrival. The early Filipino migrant community very easily assimilated to their new environments and with access to good jobs—avoided the need to take on the risks of starting small businesses entirely. Interestingly, the popularization of Filipino food now occurring in the US is predominantly led by second gen-eration Filipino Americans who are choosing to open restau-rants, in part as a means of reconnecting with and showcasing their Filipino heritage.

The second challenge for Filipino food to become known globally is that dishes are complex, vary widely and there is no consensus of what are its national dishes. Italians have pizza and pasta; the US its burgers, fries and fried chicken,

**With millions of Filipinos now living in the United States, fusion snacks like these Fil-Am sliders are gaining popularity among foodies.**

for the Japanese sushi, ramen and *tonkatsu*. But what are the iconic dishes of Filipino food? Most Filipinos would agree that *adobo* makes the list—but beyond that the answer is nuanced. Is it the Chinese influenced *lumpia* and *pancit*? Or the Spanish inspired *caldereta* or *menudo*? What about the Malay style *ginataan* dishes? Should *sinigang* or *kinilaw* be there? Where does *lechon* fit in? Then we add to this the immense regional variation that exists: is it *lumpia shanghai*, *togue*, or *hubad*? Is my *ginataan* sweet and creamy, or laced with turmeric and chilies? There is not a single answer to these questions, even among Filipinos.

The goal should be to communicate by a handful of classic recipes that define the cuisine and allow for a level of global mass adoption consumption by non-Filipinos. Just as people may not know every single type of pasta sauce from Italy, everyone basically understands what pasta is. People may not know the many different ways *adobo* can be prepared, but ideally it can become common knowledge that it normally contains pork, vinegar, soy sauce and it's from the Philippines! And it starts with Filipinos reaching a consensus among themselves.

So the last factor is around whether there is now a sufficient cadre of passionate chefs, restauranteurs and advocates packaging and marketing the food for new audiences In an interview for *Asian Traveler* magazine, Filipino chef Fernando Aracama said one reason why Filipino food isn't breaking the world stage just yet could also be because of Filipinos. "We're not proud of it. It's the opposite of pride. It's not shame, because that would be too harsh. We're apologetic. And we're apologetic about many things, especially our food. The old adages that it's oily, it's brown food … peasant food." Some even suggested that this may be due to a sense of cultural inferiority borne out of centuries of colonization. Harvard scholar Rene Orquiza has noted that "American colonial publications in the Philippines repeatedly stressed the superiority of the American diet over native foods. Immigrants to the US from the early 20th century received the message that their food was strange and unpalatable".

But there are plenty of signs that this is changing, and that there is an increasingly proud cadre or on-shore and off-shore culinary professionals, critics and food-

**The Mediterranean influences in Filipino food from the Spanish create possibilities for innovative adaptations of pasta dishes.**

ies finally coming together to showcase authentic Filipino cooking to an international standard.

The Filipino Food Movement, a not-for-profit advocacy in the US, now organizes an annual Filipino Food Festival in California each year. Its growing social media influence is now connecting Filipino food with new audiences around the world. While in cosmopolitan hotspots of the US like New York or Los Angeles, Filipino fine dining establishments such as Maharlika, Rice Bar, F.O.B. or gastropub Jeepney are earning critical acclaim.

In 2016 Filipino food landed on the list of new Gastronomic-8 in the Future of Food Report by food and beverage brand marketing communications firm, Catch on. The rationale for its inclusion was cited as: "the cross-pollination of culinary influences in Philippine cuisine mirrors the country's colorful historical influences and these influences are amplified and interpreted gastronomically for the world by a young breed of bold and tech-savvy Filipino chefs".

All this is adding up to long-coming awakening of Filipino food, which is already being heralded by forward thinking international food commentators and gourmands. Food expert Simon Majumdar, author of *Eat My Globe* and TV chef and author Anthony Bourdain had nothing but love for the Filipino cooking. Majumdar said of the fare, "the cuisine of the Philippines turned out to be a huge surprise. I underestimated how delicious Philippine food is. I think it's one of the few undiscovered culinary treasures in the world. And if the Filipinos attack the marketing of their foods, with the same gusto taken to eating it, it could be the next culinary sensation." In 2008, Bourdain famously proclaimed the Philippines' Cebu *lechon* as best whole roast pig he had tasted n the world.

In present day Manila, we're seeing a local revitalization of Filipino cooking, with a proud focus on sourcing the best seasonal ingredients, choosing local over imported goods, observing traditional cooking methods, improving presentation, and innovating dishes to give Filipino flavors greater international appeal. Ask me where I eat Filipino food in and around Manila, for traditional to the core Filipino its Abe, Pamana, or XO46, while for modern innovation on the cuisine I love Vask Gallery, Sarsa and Café Romulo.

What all these restaurants and the chefs behind them have in common is that they are Filipinos who are simply proud of their own cuisine and committed to its preparation and presentation with a razor sharp focus to quality and authenticity. These talented chefs are embracing the essence of Filipino food taking no short cuts in presenting it at its best, and ever-improving the cuisine without betraying its rich tradition and heritage. I humbly consider myself among their number through my *Maputing Cooking* blog which having discovered the treasure that it is, seeks to inter-

**The rise of video streaming online has allowed me to tell the true story of Filipino food directly to an audience around the world.**

**Filipino buffalo cheese is great with *bruschetta*, *hors doeuvres*, or this classic Sydney breakfast.**

nationalize and popularize Filipino food both in the Philippines and abroad through the digital medium to the homes of Filipinos and non-Filipinos alike. Filipinos are avid social media users, and collectively we can tell the rich story of Filipino food to a global audience online.

Lastly, I believe that the best ambassadors in promoting Filipino food are Filipinos themselves—and it starts at home. For my part I have been teaching my son since two years of age how to cook simple Filipino food. We make *ampalaya 't itlog*, *adobong kangkong*, or *giniling baboy 't sitaw*, using fresh vegetables grown on our rooftop garden. As he grows up, he too will pass on his knowledge and passion for the cuisine to others. It's through many small acts like this and measured over years, and shared with neighbors and friends around the world, that will see the true emergence of Filipino food on the global stage. If recent events are anything to judge by, this process is already well underway!

# How to Enjoy Filipino Food with Friends

For many people, trying Filipino food for the first time can be quite confronting. Characterized by unlikely flavor combinations, popularized "frankenfoods", and a history more complex than others, it takes some time, patience, and an open mind to understand this cuisine.

For me, what sets Filipino food apart is the balancing of powerful and contradicting flavors in a dish. Our taste buds are wired to register and interpret five primary tastes: salty, sweet, sour, bitter and *umami* or savoriness. While most foods show two or three of these taste sensations, many Filipino dishes comprised four or more. Consider the Visayan specialty Pork Humba, an evolution of the simple *adobo*, *humba* blends sweet (brown sugar/pineapple) with salt (soy sauce and fermented black soybeans) with sour (vinegar) and *umami* (the slow cooked pork belly) to showcase the contradictions and complexity of Filipino food.

The contrasts found in Filipino food can be extreme and challenge culinary norms: its *champorado* with *tuyo* (very sweet chocolate rice with very salty dried fish), *manggang hilaw* with *bagoong* (sour green mangoes with salty fermented shrimp paste), *puto* with *dinuguan* (a sweet rice cake, with a savory/sour blood stew) or an *ampalaya* salad (bitter gourd with sour tomatoes and calamansi juice). My own Tuna, Mango, Ampalaya salsa, lifted by salt, olive oil and calamansi juice blends all five taste sensations in a single dish. I specifically developed this to showcase the contradictions and complexity of Filipino food for non-Filipinos.

Filipino palates can be quite varied and it can be hard to cook a recipe to please everyone. Filipino cuisine has evolved to include *sawsawan*, or dipping sauces, which are used to add additional flavor to a dish according to individual preference. According to food anthropologist Doreen Fernandez, *sawsawan* is used to fine-tune the taste of the dish to the preference of the diner. Unlike in western

There are very few rules when it comes to enjoying Filipino food. Experimentation is at the very heart of the cuisine.

countries, especially in France, where the self-esteem of the chef is something people should take into consideration, Filipinos are more than fine with diners tweaking the dish's taste depending on how they like it.

There's a wide array of *sawsawan* that Filipinos use in everyday meals. Vinegar, soy sauce, *patis*, and *bagoong* are some of the common dipping sauces used, either on their own, or in simple combinations like *toyomansi*, or spiced vinegar. For example, Chicken Tinola (whole chicken in savory broth with slightly bitter chili or *malunggay* leaves) is served with *patis* (fish sauce) and calamansi to add salt and sourness to the dish.

Reflecting the complexity of the cuisine and exquisite, modern Filipino language includes a surprising number of unique terms to describe different taste sensations. Mostly having no direct English translations, Filipinos describe foods as *maango*, *mapakla*, *makunat*, *maligat*, *malansa* and *maaskad*. *Maango* means the fresh meat or milk is starting to lose its freshness; *mapakla* can be loosely translated as bitter, though in the context of fruits; *makunat* is commonly used when a food loses its crispiness or crunch; *maligat* is when a food is at its delicious consistency, glutinous; and *malansa* pertains to both smell and taste, normally associated with the smell and taste of fish.

According to Chef Claude Tayag and Mary Ann Quioc in their book *Linamnam: Eating One's Way Around the Philippines*, there is only one word to describe the Filipino cuisine: *malinamnam*. Again, this term has no direct English translation, but the closest would be "deliciousness". It could also mean flavorful, tasty, savory, and food-gasmic, it's all of the above, and more. It's the sound that you make when something is tasty, "mmmmm," "namnam".

And that is really how I have come to understand this multi-faceted cuisine. Through the centuries of culinary experimentation, the juxtaposition of unlikely food pairings, contradictions of taste sensations and powerful flavors of Filipino food are surprisingly balanced, and somehow come together as something delicious and quite exquisite.

## How to Eat Like a Filipino

The classic Filipino dining experience starts off with plates turned upside down—so they won't get dirty—patiently waiting for diners to sit down and turn it over themselves. The table is filled with different dishes, from appetizers to main dishes, to beverages down to the desserts. All are typically prepared earlier in the day and served lukewarm, or room temperature.

*Tara, kain tayo!* or "C'mon, let's eat!" is the typical signal for everyone to start eating. As a highly communal society, Filipinos never forget to make a gesture of asking everyone in the immediate vicinity to share their food even if it's not enough for more than one person. Whether the invited partakes or not with the food, it's up to them, though the polite way to decline is to answer, *Busog pa ako* or "It's okay, I'm still full."

As they take their seats Filipinos are initially somewhat indifferent of each other, *galit-galit muna* (or "upset with each other") while their attention is solely focused on filling their plates from the many different dishes on offer and starting to take their fill. Though as

This breakfast burrito is revitalizes the classic beef tapa and egg breakfast, with fresh greens, a hint of relish, and all wrapped in a corn flour tortilla.

their hunger begins to be satiated they will indulge in long and lively conversation. *Salu-salo* is a term Filipinos are all very familiar of. It means sharing meals together while enjoying each other's company. Filipinos are very sociable and they make it a point to make every event the chance to meet new people. Whether it be celebrating weddings, anniversaries, graduation parties, or wakes down to the simple meetings and get-togethers, food will always be laid on the table.

They pile their plate with everything they fancy, all at once! It doesn't matter if one dish's sauce combines with the other dishes' sauce in the process. Filipinos don't eat in courses, they go from one dish to another. From savory to sweet, then on to some soup then dessert, and back to savory again. They may eat some of their sweet *leche flan* first, before slurping down some sour *sinigang*. In restaurants, they eat whatever happens to be served first, and eat the others as second helpings with the same gusto. Desserts do not necessarily finish Filipino meals, they complement the flavors that are already on the table. This cacophony of competing flavors enjoyed at once is the principal cause of difficulty when it comes to pairing wine with Filipino food!

There are very few rules of conduct at the Filipino dining table—except that you get full—but there a few dining habits to be aware of. First, forget about knives and forks, Filipinos use forks and spoons. The use of bare hands in eating is also encouraged. Known as *kamayan*, Filipinos believe using your bare hands enhances the taste and the experience. While the case, in the modern dining establishments of Manila the practice is now increasingly rare, and as someone who prefers eating with my hands, I often find I'm the only one in the restaurant eating *kamayan*!

Filipinos are very shy to take the last piece of food from a communal plate known as the *dyahe* piece (derived from *hiya*, meaning embarrassing or shy). Often the *dyahe* piece is wasted as all diners politely decline to finish it (as a *foreign-noy* I'm able to plead cultural ignorance and I regularly get away with eating the *dyahe*!). It also makes sense to leave a last morsel of food on one's own plate, as visible proof that one is so full they cannot eat another mouthful. A clean plate is likely to be met by eager prompts of *sige pa, kain ka pa*, literally "come on, you eat some more".

Rice is the essential and ever present staple of the Filipino diet. For Filipinos, not eating rice is tantamount to not eating at all. It is the mild flavored backdrop that adds substance and elevates the flavors of *ulam* paired with it. Even without the hearty dishes, rice is often consumed on its own with just a little *bagoong* or salt. According to Doreen Fernandez, the word rice has over two hundred words related to it. Some of the common terms include *bigas*, *kanin*, *tutong*, *palay*, *galapong*, *kiping*, *malagkit*, and *pinipig*. The diverse lexicon is reflective of the myriad of ways rice can be prepared and consumed in Filipino cooking.

Breakfast, considered the most important meal of the day, is still most commonly served with rice. While Filipinos won't pass on freshly cooked steamed rice, nothing beats *sinangag* for breakfast. *Sinangag* or garlic fried rice, is prepared using leftover rice to prevent it from spoiling, revitalized with a little garlic, onions, salt, pepper and oil. Leftover rice is key to a delicious *sinangag*.

*Sinangag* is paired with a lot of viands particularly cured, dried or fried meats. When a fried egg is tossed in the mix, it forms the ultimate breakfast trifecta: the *silog*. The Philippines' answer to the American Breakfast, the original concoction was known as *tapsilog*, a portmanteau of the words TAPa, SInangag and itLOG. Over the years, the repertoire of breakfast options expanded to include *longsilog* (*longganisa*), *chicksilog* (cured chicken), *bangsilog* (fried *bangus* or milk fish), *tosilog* (*tocino* or cured pork) and *hotsilog* (fried hotdogs) among others.

Rice is also the main ingredient in some well-loved Filipino recipes like *goto*, *arroz caldo*, *bringhe*, *champorado* and *kakanin* further stamping its mark as central to the Filipino life. Rice wines are also prevalent particularly in the mountainous Cordilleras region; while even rice "coffee" exists in the Philippines believed to treat stomachache. Rice is also basis of *kakanin*—the name given to the many tyes of sweetened native rice cakes typically comprised of rice, cassava, camote, and *ube* and usually served as *merienda*. There are literally as many ways to consume rice in the Philippines as there are meals in the day, so to eat like a Filipino is to eat a whole lot of rice—you have been warned!

To say that Filipinos love eating is an understatement. Generally, Filipinos eat five to six meals a day. There's breakfast, morning snack at 10am, lunch, afternoon snack at 4pm, supper, and for those who still need to satiate their cravings, they can always have midnight snack.

Wherever you are in the Philippines and whatever the time of day, one thing you may be certain of is that your next meal is not far away. It is a nation quite literally obsessed with food. When eating like a Filipino you will always have fun and always be full.

**Even seemingly simple Filipino fare is deceptively complex in flavor. Sweet and sour *atchara* will bring life to salty smoked fish.**

# The Fundamentals of Filipino Cooking

Prior to the arrival of external culinary techniques, indigenous Philippine cooking revolved around four simple techniques: boiling, steaming, roasting and grilling.

Food like fish and seafood are often cooked in indigenous ways. Meat, on the other hand, is cooked both ways, indigenous and indigenized ways, the way Spanish, Chinese and Americans cooked their food. This implies that meat were introduced in the country at a later time, as influenced by foreign cultures.

Boiling is one of the main methods of cooking and is the basis of many Filipino recipes. Nilagang Baka or boiled beef soup for instance is even named after this cooking method (*laga* being the root word "to boil"). The long boiling process makes tough cuts of meat soft and imparts a rich flavor to the broth. In *sinigang* souring agents like *sampaloc, bayabas, kamias* and calamansi are boiled with the vegetables, seafood or meat to impart their sour flavor to the tasty broth. *Bulalo*, on the other hand, uses a cow's leg bone and boiled for hours until the marrow and cartilage in the beef are rendered soft and palatable.

Steaming or *halabos* is one of the best cooking methods that maximize the taste and flavor of a dish. Seafood is most commonly steamed and yields delicious results with tender skin and the flesh springy to the bite.

**In Filipino food, unlikely pairs like seaweed and unripe fruits come together in the same bowl combined into something delicious.**

Roasting over open fires or in pits is one of the less common, but still iconic, cooking methods found in the Philippines. *Lechon* is a meaty, fatty, crisp, red-skinned whole pig roasted to perfection. *Lechon* is the quintessential fiesta fare. A dish to be eaten in moderation, but there is something about its glistening golden brown skin in oil and aroma that makes one forget their diet.

Grilling is another foundation of cooking Filipino food. Pre-burnt coconut husks or charcoals are used for grilling with the temperature controlled by vigorous fanning using a traditional fan or *pamaypay*. Sliced pork are skewered on a bamboo stick and made into classic pork barbecue, while chicken breasts, thighs and wings are threaded in bigger sticks and are called chicken *inasal*. Innards—like intestines, chicken heads and feet, coagulated blood—are also popular when chargrilled.

*Ginataan* literally means to cook something in coconut milk, which makes the food richer in flavor and creamier in texture. *Gata*-based dishes can incorporate seafood like crab, chicken, pork or vegetables like squash and green beans.

These simple, low tech cooking styles yielded improved results when coupled with natural techniques that could enhance the dishes' flavor. Cooking in claypots or wood-fired ovens adds texture and flavor, while wrapping foods in banana leaves, bamboo leaves, pandan leaves and taro leaves enhance the flavor and aroma. Green bamboo tubes can be used as a vessel to cook rice which imparts interesting new flavors.

Before the modern era of refrigeration, earlier generations of Filipinos needed to find ways to prolong the lifespan of food. This necessity gave rise to a range of cooking methods that now characterize Filipino food such as *adobo, kinilaw, paksiw* and the drying or smoking of food.

*Adobo* is typically associated with the Spanish culinary arts, however it is believed cooking in vinegar predated the

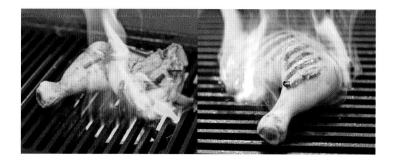

**Grilling over open fire, or hot coals imparts burnt and smoky notes that add a new dimension to cooking.**

flavorings. Sautéing is considered an elite way of cooking since olive oil was an expensive commodity during the Spanish era. Today, sautéing is a common form of cooking in Filipino homes with the range of cooking oils available in the market.

With the American influence on Filipino culinary arts in the 20th century, modern appliances are now also widely used in Filipino cooking. Pressure cookers, microwaves, electric blenders and food processors are widely used to save cooking time—especially when it comes to tenderizing meats.

Spanish colonial period. *Adobong puti* (white adobo) is the most primitive form of *adobo*, in essence cooking in vinegar and garlic only. While there are as many recipes for *adobo* as there are Filipino families, the classic Filipino *adobo* typically combines vinegar and soy sauce with bay leaves, garlic, onions and peppercorns.

*Kilawin* or *kinilaw* is another method of cooking that is also popular as a dish on its own. *Kilawin* is the Philippines' version to Spain's *ceviche*. Raw fish and shrimp are slowly "cooked" in the vinegar's acid—sometimes referred to as liquid fire. Salt and pepper are added to taste, while flavors can be enhanced further with the addition of chilies and calamansi. Filipino food historian Doreen Fernandez suggests that *kinilaw* may be one of the most ancient Philippine food and method that exists.

The third kind of preserving food is called *paksiw*, which refers to the cooking of fish or meats in vinegar and other condiments, usually simmering until the pan is dry and the resulting meat begins to fry. Cooked this way, and incorporating the vinegar, the food may be served either hot or cold for days afterwards.

Sun-drying of food is widely practiced in many regions. *Pagdadaing*, as it is known, is done to prevent fish from spoiling. Large fish like milkfish are split open, salted, and dried in the sun and are called *daing*, small fishes are salted whole and dried and are called *tuyo*. Other ways fish is preserved is through smoking until they turn golden brown and are called *tinapa*.

Sautéing and frying were only introduced during the Spanish period. Pork, beef and fish dishes would be fried in olive oil, and enhanced with wine and other European

# Unique Ingredients Used in Filipino Cooking

While Philippine cuisine has influences from around the world, and through the integration of ingredients from Spanish, Mexican, Chinese and American, they have become common ingredients in the Filipino cooking as well. However, in this section, we'll focus on exploring those ingredients that are iconic or indigenous to Filipino cooking. Some of the local ingredients used in the recipes are annatto seeds (*atsuete*), fermented shrimp or fish paste (*bagoong*), banana heart (*puso ng saging*), bitter gourd (*ampalaya*), chilies (*sili*), coconut and its by-products *nata de  coco* and *macapuno*, calamansi, *dayap*, *dalandan*, Filipino salted egg (*itlog na maalat*), taro (*gabi*), kangkong, *malunggay*, tamarind (*sampaloc*), bilimbi (*kamias*), pandan leaves, and lemongrass (*tanglad*).

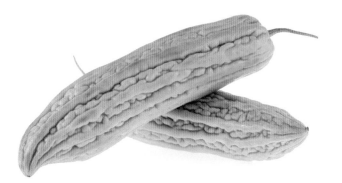

Ampalaya or bitter gourd is a vegetable with a bitter taste and wrinkled skin. Its size ranges from three inches to ten inches (7 cm–25 cm) in length. If a less bitter *ampalaya* is preferred, choose one that has larger "wrinkle" gaps. The larger the gaps, the less bitter the *ampalaya* will be. When eaten raw, the bitterness can be overpowering. To remove the bitterness, slice the gourd in small pieces and soak them in salted water. Rinse before cooking.

Annatto seeds or *atsuete* are dried, reddish-brown seeds that are used as a natural food coloring or dye. The seeds are soaked first in warm water or fried in oil for a few minutes until desired color is achieved. Strain the liquid and discard the seeds. The liquid can now be used for cooking *kare-kare* (a traditional Philippine stew) and for basting roasted chicken (*inasal*) giving them their distinct hint of orange color. Annatto seeds can easily be bought in supermarkets, and are sometimes labeled as "achiote". You can substitute annatto seeds with turmeric or paprika, or mixture of the two.

**Banana heart**, also known as banana blossom or *puso ng saging* is the innermost portion of the banana flower. A textural and filling vegetable, it's popular to include in pork *humba*, or cooked in coconut milk with other vegetables. To prepare, remove several layers of the hard outer sheets to reveal the lighter colored inner layers. Cut into thin circles or quarters and soak them in salted water before cooking. Easily available fresh in local Philippines market, the bottled or canned versions can be found in Asian grocery stores. Artichoke hearts or zucchini flowers may be used as substitutes.

**Banana ketchup** looks like regular ketchup and is made from bananas, tomatoes, sugar, vinegar and spices. It's used as a basting sauce or dipping sauce. You'll find bottled banana ketchup in the condiments section of Asian supermarkets and grocery stores.

**Bilimbi** or *kamias* is a small, green vegetable that resembles a mini cucumber, but grows on a tree. Highly sour, it is also a common souring agent in *sinigang*, or added to certain curries, or coconut based stews. This ingredient can be extremely hard to find outside of the Philippines, but it does grow in sub-tropical climates. Ask around your local Filipino community, it's likely some Filipino neighbors will have *kamias* trees in their backyards and happy to share some of their harvest.

**Calamansi** are small citrus fruits with a flavor somewhere between a lime and an orange. It is used widely in the Philippines in drinks, dipping sauce, marinades or as a souring agent in soups. Key limes can be used as substitute for calamansi, or regular limes as a last resort. The Philippines is also home to larger citrus fruits, similar to oranges or mandarin, *dayap* and *dalandan* are used to add flavors to desserts or in drinks.

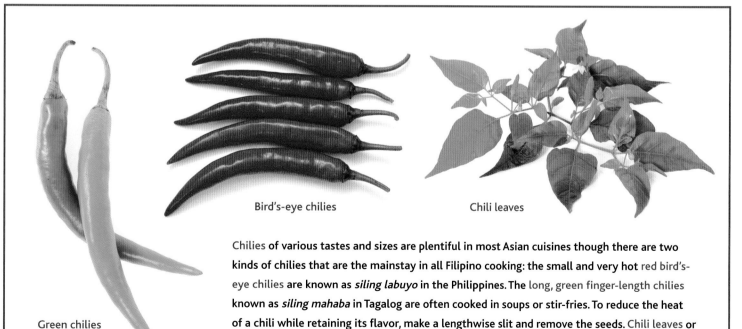

Bird's-eye chilies

Chili leaves

Green chilies

**Chilies** of various tastes and sizes are plentiful in most Asian cuisines though there are two kinds of chilies that are the mainstay in all Filipino cooking: the small and very hot red bird's-eye chilies are known as *siling labuyo* in the Philippines. The long, green finger-length chilies known as *siling mahaba* in Tagalog are often cooked in soups or stir-fries. To reduce the heat of a chili while retaining its flavor, make a lengthwise slit and remove the seeds. Chili leaves or *dahon ng sili* are commonly used in Filipino cooking—in stews or curries.

Coconuts are abundant in the Philippines. This is one of the fruits where almost all parts are utilized, in different ways depending on the age of the coconut. A young, freshly picked coconut is called *buko*, and the fresh *buko* juice can be consumed as a refreshing drink or used in soups and cooking. The young flesh is used in desserts including *buko* pie. In non-tropical countries, coconut juice can be found packed in bottles and tetra packs and are sold in grocery stores.

Older coconuts where the shell and meat have hardened are known as *niyog*. The hard white flesh is ground and pressed to extract coconut cream or *kakang gata* which is widely used in Filipino cooking. Coconut cream and coconut milk are used in many Filipino desserts and curries. To obtain fresh coconut cream, grate the flesh of 1 coconut into a bowl (this yields about 3 cups of grated coconut flesh), add ½ cup water and knead thoroughly a few times, then squeeze the mixture firmly in your fist or strain with a muslin cloth or cheese cloth. Thick coconut milk is obtained by the same method but by adding double the water to the grated flesh (about 1 cup instead of ½ cup). Thin coconut milk is obtained by pressing the grated coconut a second time—adding 1 cup of water to the same grated coconut flesh and squeezing it again. Although freshly pressed milk has more flavor, coconut cream and milk are now widely sold canned or in packets that are quick, convenient and quite tasty. Canned or packet coconut cream or milk comes in varying consistencies depending on the brand, and you will need to try them out and adjust the thickness by adding water as needed.

Coriander leaves, also known as cilantro, are widely used as a flavoring and garnish. Fresh coriander leaves have a strong taste and aroma and can be refrigerated in a plastic bag for about a week. Parsley is a suitable substitute.

Fermented black soybeans (*taosi*), also called salted black beans have a strong salty, pungent and slightly bitter flavor. *Taosi* is often used in braising meats or steaming fish. They are sold in small cans in most Asian grocery stores.

Fermented shrimp or fish paste (*bagoong*) is used as *sawsawan* or dipping sauce, though it is also used in cooking to impart saltiness and a robust seafood flavor to a dish. *Bagoong alamang*, derived from baby shrimp is usually paired with *kare-kare*, or coconut based curries like *laing*, or coconut cooked vegetables. *Bagoong alamang* can be spicy and sweet as well, depending on the diner's preference. *Bagoong isda* on the other hand

is a kind of *bagoong* made from fish, typically *dilis* (anchovies). This is usually used to add flavor to the vegetable medley *pinakbet* and dishes like enchiladas. *Bagoong balayan* is made from fermented anchovies and round scad but it is a thin liquid sauce instead of a paste. Fresh *bagoong* can be bought in wet markets in the Philippines, or in preserved, ready to eat form in supermarkets and Asian grocery stores around the world. Depending on the dish, other salty condiments like fish sauce or soy sauce can be substituted.

Fish sauce (*patis*) is a very salty, translucent, amber-colored fermented sauce that is available in bottles. There are many brands in the market. An essential ingredient in Filipino cooking, fish sauce is either used as a seasoning when cooking or used as a dipping sauce. Fish sauce made in Vietnam, Thailand and China are very similar and are good substitutes.

Green papaya or unripe papaya is a pear-shaped fruit commonly found in Southeast Asia but is often used as a vegetable in Philippine cooking. It's the key ingredient in *Atchara*, a sweet and sour pickle Filipinos love pairing with grilled pork, and as accompaniment in *tinolang manok*. It's available year round and tastes more sour than it is sweet depending how unripe it is when cooked.

Glutinous rice (*malagkit*) in the Philippines is normally used to make desserts. This type of rice turns sticky when cooked. It is sold in Asian grocery stores and supermarkets.

Gulaman, widely known elsewhere as agar, refers to the dried bar of seaweed used to make a variety of Filipino drinks and desserts. It comes in different colors and should not be confused with gelatin. While the two look alike, gelatin is a protein and *gulaman* is a carbohydrate derived from seaweed. Gelatin also dissolves in hot water while *gulaman* dissolves in boiling water. Gelatin can be used as a substitute for gulaman in *sago't gulaman*, a cold, sweet, refreshing drink sold in the streets of Manila.

*Kesong puti* is a soft, unaged, white cheese made from unskimmed carabao's milk, salt, and rennet. This cheese originated from and is produced in the provinces of Bulacan, Cebu, Laguna, Bacolod and Samar. In the Philippines, it is a popular breakfast fare eaten with the freshly baked local bread called *pan de sal*.

Noodles can be made from rice or wheat flour or mung beans. *Pancit* is a generic term used to refer to a noodle dish. There is a wide range of noodles, and each type has a different texture and taste. Always follow the package instructions when cooking noodles. Glass noodles (*sotanghon*), also known as transparent mung bean noodles or cellophane noodles, are dried and white colored. Glass noodles need to be soaked in water before they are added to the pan. The noodles turn transparent when cooked. They can be stir-fried or cooked in soups. Wheat noodles commonly come in four types. Canton noodles are dried, round and yellow in color. They may be quickly scalded in hot water to soften or added at the last minute to pan as these noodles cook easily. This noodle is a good choice for stir-fry dishes. Mami noodles, or Chinese egg noodles, are normally made of flour and eggs. They are thin, often dried and yellow in color. Miki noodles are thick, wide and normally flat yellow colored noodles. They are a perfect for soups. They are sometimes called "Shanghai noodles". Misua is a dried, thin, white-colored noodle with a glossy, smooth texture. They cook quickly and are a good choice for soups.

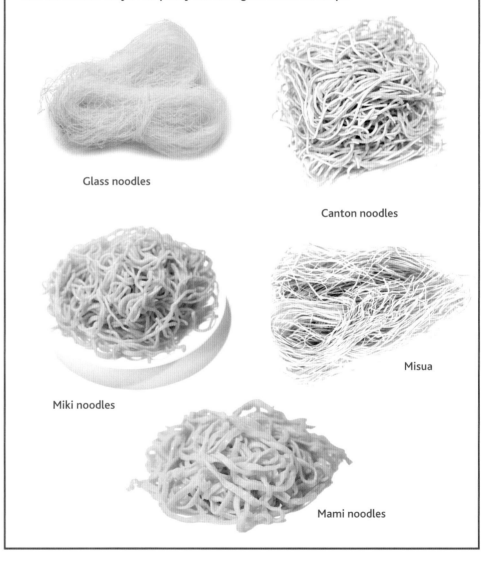

Glass noodles

Canton noodles

Miki noodles

Misua

Mami noodles

mussels. They are sold alongside fresh eggs in markets but are relatively harder to find abroad since its shelf life may only last for two to four weeks, depending on the process done to cook it. The good thing is salted eggs are very easy to make at home by soaking the eggs in brine solution or coating the eggs with clay and salt mixture.

Lemongrass or *tanglad* also gives a rousing aroma to foods from its long stalk. A hardy perennial grass plant, it's easy to cultivate at home. In cooking, it enhances the flavor of the meat and is typically used in *lechon* or as a flavoring agent for chicken dishes such as *tinola*, or chicken *inasal*. It is prepared by bruising the stalk usually a few times with the back of a knife blade to release the flavor in cooking. Fresh ginger combined with lemon zest is the best substitute when lemongrass is unavailable.

Pandan leaves are long fragrant leaf from the *pandanus* plant that gives a unique fragrance to various food. It is used in steaming rice and enhancing flavors of meat and even desserts and drinks. It can also be used as a natural coloring agent.

*Pan de sal* is the national bread of the Philippines, usually made with salt, yeast, sugar and flour and shaped into a bun. Substitute any bread or bun of your choice.

Salted eggs (*itlog na maalat*), or a salted duck egg, is a savory condiment or side dish that has been boiled, stored in brine and dyed red. They are painted red to distinguish it from the basic hard boiled egg and avoid confusion. They are delicious when served with fresh tomatoes to cut the powerful flavor or can be used as the backbone of richly flavored sauces often paired with shrimp, lobster or

Originating from China, soy sauce is a deep brown dipping sauce made from fermented soy beans with wheat and salt. Locally known as *toyo*, this is one of the typical condiments found in the Filipino kitchen. It is one of the two main ingredient of the famous Filipino dish *adobo*, the other being vinegar. *Toyo* is a popular dipping sauce paired with different spices and ingredients like calamansi, vinegar, pepper, tomato, garlic, and onion. Some of the usual soy sauce-spice combinations are: *toyomansi*, compound word for "*toyo*" and "calamansi," *toyomansi* with *siling labuyo* (bird's-eye chili), and *toyo, suka, sili* (soy sauce, vinegar, and bird's-eye chili).

*Malunggay* or moringa is a popular plant in the Philippines known as a good source of vitamins and a herbal medicine. It is typically used as a vegetable in *tinolang manok* and because it is rich in nutrients, it is also incorporated in other food like *pan de sal* thus giving birth to *malunggay pan de sal*. It can also be brewed as a herbal tea. Lactating moms are advised to eat food that has *malunggay* as an ingredient to help them produce more milk for babies.

Tamarind (*sampaloc*) is one of the popular souring agents used in *sinigang*. A dark brown pod containing seeds, it is prepared by boiling the pods until soft, then crushing, them and straining to release their juice. While tamarind flavored sachet powders are widely available, they often contain artificial additives, so keep an eye out for fresh tamarind at Asian grocery stores if you can. Tamarind leaves are available in both fresh and dried form. The fresh ones should have light green color and the leaves should not be wilted. Check the best before date before buying dried leaves.

Taro leaves or *dahon ng gabi* are used as a vegetable and is the main ingredient in cooking *laing*, a coconut curry which features taro leaves. Fresh taro leaves are itchy to the mouth, so they need to be sundried before cooking them. The taro root (*gabi*) is often used in soups as a starchy root crop that can give weight to a dish.

Ube or purple yam is a popular ingredient used in many desserts in the Philippines. Known for its highly pigmented purple color, this tuber is different from other yams as it has a deeper shade of purple and rougher-looking skin. While *ube* is commonly found in other Asian countries, in the Philippines, *ube* is typically used in jams, cakes, ice cream, and candies, but is most popular in a beloved Filipino dessert called *ube halaya*, a sweet local jam usually bought as souvenir from Baguio. It can be eaten on its own or as a special topping for *halo-halo*, a shaved ice dessert in the country.

Vinegar, also known as *suka* or native vinegar, comes in black, red and white hues. It is made from nipa palm, coconut, sago palm as well as from sugar cane. White vinegar can be used for the recipes in this book. Cane vinegar is an important ingredient in Filipino cooking. Filipino vinegar is less acidic than most vinegars used in the West. The best substitutes are white vinegar, white wine vinegar or cider vinegar.

Water spinach or *kangkong* is a green leafy vegetable used in *sinigang* or cooked on its own as *adobo*. Highly versatile, it can be added to a range of vegetable stir fries, soups, or prepared on its own either with simple garlic and chili or *adobo* style. *Kangkong* can be bought in the vegetable aisle in markets. In cooking, the leaves are picked and some soft parts of the stem can also be cooked.

# Sauces and Condiments

Filipino cuisine leaves a lot of flexibility to alter the flavor of a dish at the table according to one's own taste. This is done through commonly serving strong flavored sauces or condiments with more subtle flavored *ulam* or *viands*.

Favorite condiments include vinegar, soy sauce, fish sauce, calamansi juice, chili, garlic, tomato sauce and *bagoong*. These are often combined together to create a more complex blend of flavors that bursts in one's mouth and these are vinegar with chili (sour/spicy), vinegar or calamansi with soy sauce (sour/salty), vinegar with garlic (sour/savory), fish sauce with chili (salty/spicy), pickled papaya/vegetables (sweet/sour).

# Cooked Fermented Shrimp Paste Bagoong

*Bagoong* is a Filipino condiment made from fermented fish or shrimp. During the fermentation process, the liquid byproduct that forms on top is what we call our *patis* or Fish Sauce—which is essentially a fish steeped brine. The *bagoong* is the remaining fermented fish or shrimp material. This can be added to cooking in its "raw" form, or cooked and preserved for long term use in jars as per the recipe below. It's extremely popular when paired with sour green mangoes, and a popular condiment added to dishes like *kare-kare*, or eaten on top of steamed white rice.

**Good for 2 medium sized jars (makes 12 oz/300–400g)**
**Prep time: 10 minutes**
**Cooking time: 20 minutes**

2 tablespoons cooking oil
¼ cup (35 g) finely chopped garlic
¼ cup (40 g) finely chopped onion
1 tablespoon grated ginger
½ cup (170 g) finely chopped pork fat
½ lb (250 g) fermented shrimp paste (*bagoong alamang*)
¼ cup (60 ml) vinegar
¼ cup (60 ml) water
¼ cup (50 g) brown sugar
2–3 red bird's-eye chilies (*siling labuyo*), optional

**1.** In a shallow skillet, heat the oil and sauté the garlic until lightly toasted. Add the onions and ginger and sauté until fragrant.
**2.** Follow it up with the pork fat and let it release its fat or until it turns golden brown. Then mix in the shrimp paste until it changes color to a dark brown.
**3.** Deglaze the pan with vinegar and water. Then mix in the brown sugar until it dissolves and caramelizes. Add the chilies, if using, and let it simmer for another 5 minutes.
**4.** Let it cool while you prepare the jars to store the *bagoong*. Ensure the jars are properly sterilized by either boiling or heating them in the oven. Transfer the cooked *bagoong* mixture to the jars and seal tightly.

# Sweet Liver Sauce
## Sarsa ng Lechon

Lechon sauce is a liver based gravy that is served with roast meats, especially the whole roast pig or *lechon*. It is simultaneously sweet, savory, rich and textured—and takes roast pork to new heights of decadence! While it's nice to prepare it from scratch using raw livers, you can save a lot of time by starting with a good quality liver spread, or pate.

**Good for 3 cups (750 ml)**
**Prep time: 10 minutes**
**Cooking time: 25 minutes**

½ lb (250 g) liver (pork, chicken, or a combination of both)
½ cup (125 ml) vinegar
¼ cup (60 ml) cooking oil
3 tablespoons chopped garlic
½ cup (80 g) chopped onion
2 cups (500 ml) chicken stock or water
½ cup (100 g) brown sugar
¼ cup (60 ml) soy sauce
3 bay leaves
½ cup (30 g) bread crumbs (old *pan de sal* or *monay*)
Salt and pepper, to taste

1. In a small pot, blanch the liver in boiling water for 5–10 minutes or until half cooked. Transfer them with tongs into a blender. Blend it well in moderate setting while slowly adding in the vinegar until everything is smooth and pureed. Set aside.
2. In a shallow skillet, heat the oil and sauté the garlic and onion on medium heat until fragrant. Add the liver mixture, chicken stock, brown sugar, soy sauce and bay leaves. Let it simmer for 10 minutes and stir occasionally.
3. Gradually add the bread crumbs while continuously stirring to avoid any lumps.
4. Season with salt and pepper and let it simmer for 5 minutes on medium heat until the sauce becomes thick.
5. Serve with roast or grilled pork (*lechon* or *liempo*)

# Soy Sauce, Vinegar, and Chili Dipping Sauce
## Toyo Suka at Sili

Toyo Suka At Sili is a favorite condiment when eating something grilled, fatty and savory. Grilled Pork Belly (*Inihaw na liempo*) and Pork Barbecue are the perfect dishes to try with this dipping sauce. The vinegar cuts through the grease leaving you wanting to eat more and more.

**Good for ½ cup (125 ml)**
**Prep time: 15 minutes**
**No cooking needed**

¼ cup (60 ml) vinegar
¼ cup (60 ml) soy sauce
1 teaspoon sugar
2 tablespoons minced garlic
2 tablespoons chopped onion
½ teaspoon pepper
2–3 red bird's-eye chilies (*siling labuyo*), chopped

1. In a small mixing bowl, combine the vinegar, soy sauce and sugar. Mix until the sugar is completely dissolved. Add the garlic, onion, pepper and chilies. Add as much chilies as you want to achieve desired level of spiciness.
2. Let the spices infuse the sauce and let it sit for 10 minutes before serving.
3. Transfer to a sauce dish and serve with grilled pork or chicken.

# Filipino Style Spiced Vinegar

There are lots of versions for spiced vinegar in the Philippines. We have the *sukang tuba*, *sukang Iloko*, *sinamak*, *pinakurat* and many more. What makes each one different is the spices they include and the type of vinegar used. Some uses sugar cane (cane vinegar), coconut palm (*sukang tuba*) or even nipa sap (*sukang sasa*). I make a few bottles at a time using recycled wine bottles and corks from around the house. Besides the classic spicing agents of garlic, chili and pepper, I like mine with a hint of cucumber (*pipino*).

**Makes 6 cups (1.5 l)**
**Prep time: 15 minutes**
**Cooking time: 10 minutes**

6 cups (1.5 l) cane vinegar
1 tablespoon salt
2 tablespoons sugar
¼ cup (35 g) thinly sliced garlic
1 cup (150 g) sliced onion
¼ cup (40 g) red bird's-eye chilies (*siling labuyo*), halved
¼ cup (50 g) black peppercorns, cracked
1 cup (130 g) peeled and chopped cucumber

1. In a large glass or ceramic bowl, mix together the vinegar, salt and sugar. Stir until the sugar and salt are fully dissolved.
2. In a small bowl, mix the garlic, onion, chilies, black pepper and cucumber and divide into 2 equal parts.
3. Prepare two clean and sterilized bottles and put the combination of dry ingredients inside each bottle.
4. Fill each bottle with the vinegar mixture; use a funnel to prevent spillage. Cover with lid and let stand for 2–3 days to allow the flavors to develop before using.

# Filipino Chicken Gravy

Gravy and roast or fried chicken go hand in hand and in the Philippines this is no exception. The key difference to the gravy found in North America or Europe is the use of soy sauce for the salty agent, which gives it a more oriental feel. When having classic fried chicken, I like to mix the gravy with tomato ketchup—this gives sweetness and some extra tang.

**Good for 2 cups (500 ml)**
**Prep time: 5 minutes**
**Cooking time: 15 minutes**

3 tablespoons butter
2 teaspoons chopped garlic
¼ cup (40 g) chopped onion
2 tablespoons flour
2 cups (500 ml) chicken stock
2 tablespoons soy sauce
Salt and pepper, to taste
¼ cup (60 ml) cream

1. In a shallow skillet, melt the butter and sauté the garlic and onion on medium heat. Once fragrant, add the flour and cook for 2 minutes.
2. Gradually add the stock and stir continuously to avoid forming of lumps. Let it simmer for 5–8 minutes on low fire or until thick.
3. Add the soy sauce and season with salt and pepper.
4. Turn off the heat and add the cream. Stir to combine the cream and sauce properly.
5. Serve with Filipino fried chicken, like my Filipino Crispy Fried Chicken (Kaligayahaan Ng Manok), page 102.

# PICKLED PAPAYA
## ATCHARA

Filipinos have pickled different fruits and vegetables for centuries as one of the ways to preserve food. In atchara, grated green papaya is pickled in vinegar and sugar along with other seasonal vegetables for extra color and flavor. Atchara is often served as a relish with grilled or fried meats, especially pork, as the acidity of the vinegar cuts the fats and oils, for a more balanced taste and cleaner taste.

**Good for 2 medium sized jars (makes 3 cups/500–600g)**
**Prep time: 1 hour 30 minutes**
**Cooking time: 20 minutes**

2 cups (365 g) grated green papaya
1 tablespoon salt
2 cups (500 ml) vinegar
1 cup (200 g) sugar
10 cloves garlic, sliced thinly
2 tablespoons ginger, sliced into strips
1 carrot, cut into long thin strips (matchsticks)
5 shallots, peeled and halved
2 red and green bell peppers, cut into long thin strips
   (matchsticks)

1.  In a medium-sized mixing bowl, combine the grated papaya and salt. Let it stand for 1 hour or until the papaya starts to release its liquid. With your hands, squeeze the grated papaya as hard as you can to fully remove excess water. Discard the water and set the papaya aside.
2.  In a small casserole, boil the vinegar and sugar on medium heat. Stir occasionally until the sugar is fully dissolved. Blanch the vegetables for 2–3 minutes and set aside.

3.  In a medium-sized bowl, combine the papaya and the blanched vegetables. Toss gently to combine all ingredients.
4.  Prepare to clean and sterilize the jars. Put the grated papaya and blanched vegetables in the clean and sterilized jars. Pour in the pickling solution and seal the jar properly. Use plastic lids ideally to avoid potential corrosion from the vinegar.
5.  Cure the Atchara for 5–7 days in the refrigerator to allow the flavors to develop before eating.

# Soy and Calamansi Dipping Sauce Toyomansi

Toyomansi is an abbreviation of *toyo* (soy sauce) and calamansi. One of the most common dipping sauces found in the Philippines, it is usually paired with grilled seafood and poultry. The citrus-fruity taste of the calamansi gives you a salty but refreshing sour taste that complements the smokiness taste of your grilled dishes.

**Good for ½ cup (125 ml)**
**Prep time: 10 minutes**
**No cooking needed**

¼ cup (60 ml) calamansi juice
¼ cup (60ml) soy sauce
2 teaspoons minced garlic
2 red bird's-eye chilies (*siling labuyo*), chopped

1. With a small knife, cut the calamansi in half and squeeze the juice into a small mixing bowl. You can strain the juice if you want to remove the seeds.
2. In the same mixing bowl, mix in the soy sauce, garlic and red chilies and stir. You can add more chilies for extra spicy kick.
3. Allow to infuse for 10 minutes then transfer to a sauce dish. Serve with grilled seafood or spooned over rice.

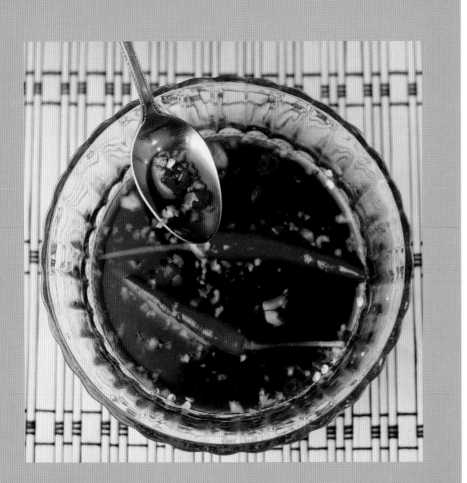

# Filipino Style Eggplant and Tomato Salad Ensaladang Talong at Kamatis

Roasted eggplants and fresh tomatoes come together in this quick and easy to make salad (*ensalada*). It is used as an accompaniment and dip for grilled and fried dishes as it cuts the grease and oil—and is often served with the meat/vegetable medley known as *pochero*. Though it's actually substantial enough it could be matched with some toasted pita bread, or crackers as a quick appetizer.

**Good for 6–8 as a side dish**
**Prep time: 20 minutes**
**Cooking time: 10 minutes**

6 medium sized long, thin eggplants
   (*talong*)
½ cup (75 g) thinly sliced onion
1 cup (200 g) tomato, cut into chunks
2 long green chilies (*siling mahaba*),
   sliced thinly
¼ cup (60 ml) vinegar
1 tablespoon sugar
Salt and pepper, to taste

1. Prepare and wash the eggplants. Lay
the eggplants directly over a gas stove
on high fire and roast for 3–5 minutes or
until soft and the skin is burnt. Turn it over
occasionally to cook it evenly. Let it cool
and peel off the skin. Chop the eggplant
into chunks and set aside.
2. In a small mixing bowl, mix together
the onion, tomato, chilies and eggplant.
Add the vinegar, sugar and season with
salt and pepper. Toss everything together
until all the flavors are mixed evenly.
3. Chill in the refrigerator for 10–15
minutes and serve cold. Best served
with pork and beef stew with bananas
(*pochero*).

# Tomato Onion Salsa KBL
## Kamatis, Bagoong, Lasona

KBL is an acronym meaning tomato (*kamatis*), fermented fish paste (*bagoong*) and
shallots (*lasona*) and is the traditional dipping sauce for the Ilocano dish
known as *Bagnet*—a chopped, crisp fried pork belly. On its own, some may find
it too fishy but when paired with the heavy, greasy *bagnet*, it flavors the meat
and provides a refreshing finish to each bite. *Lasona* is the Ilocano term for
shallots, though of course you can substitute onion leeks, or some red onion if
you don't have any available.

**Good for 2 cups (450 g)**
**Prep time: 10 minutes**
**Cooking time: No cooking needed**

1 cup (200 g) diced tomatoes
¼ cup (25 g) thinly sliced shallots (*lasona*)
1 tablespoon grated ginger
2 tablespoons chopped green onions (scallions)
¼ cup (60 ml) fermented fish paste
   (*bagoong balayan*)
2 tablespoons calamansi juice
2–3 red bird's-eye chilies (*siling labuyo*), chopped

1. In a medium-sized bowl,
combine all the ingredients and mix
them together until all flavors are
incorporated well.
2. Place in the refrigerator and chill
for 30 minutes. Transfer to sauce
dishes and serve with your favorite
*bagnet* (crisp fried pork belly) or any
fried food.

# Homemade Ketchup

Ketchup is a popular sauce in the Philippines as it adds sweetness and sour tang to any dish. It's the dipping sauce of choice for fried chicken, or fried spring rolls (*lumpiang shanghai*)—and popular at breakfast with eggs, or *tortang talong*. In the Philippines people mostly use store bought ketchup—and banana ketchup is a popular alternative, which uses bananas instead of tomatoes, though it's still colored red through the use of food coloring. As a foreign chef, I often find local factory sauces too sweet, so I normally whip up my own which can be done in a few minutes with ingredients readily available in the pantry—you just need fresh cherry tomatoes.

**Good for 1 cup (250 ml)**
**Prep time: 5 minutes**
**Cooking time: 5 minutes**

¼ cup (60 ml) olive oil
1 clove garlic, minced
2 cups (300 g) cherry
   tomatoes or regular ripe
   tomatoes, chopped
2 tablespoons cane vinegar
1 tablespoon raw sugar
Salt and pepper, to taste

1. In a shallow skillet, heat the olive oil and sauté the garlic and tomatoes on medium heat. Simmer for 2–3 minutes or until the tomatoes are softened. Toss occasionally and slightly mash the tomatoes breaking it down into chunks and releasing the tomato juices.
2. Deglaze the pan with vinegar. Add the sugar and salt and pepper to taste
3. Keep the sauce chunky and this can be served while still hot. Best served with Roasted Eggplant Torta (page 80) "Shangai" Spring Rolls (page 41) and Filipino Crispy Fried Chicken (page 102).

# Fermented Fish and Calamansi Sauce Bagoong Isda at Suka o Calamansi

Bagoong Isda is made from fermented anchovies or other small fish in brine. Salty, fishy and pungent, the vinegar or calamansi contrasts the salt with sourness and makes the *bagoong* a bit more palatable (similar to when it is paired with green mango). This dipping sauce is very popular in the provinces, where it is paired with simple local fare, such as boiled vegetables like okra, eggplant, string beans, winged beans (*sigarilyas*)—and of course steamed rice.

**Good for ½ cup (120 ml)**
**Prep time: 10 minutes**
**Cooking time: No cooking needed**

# Streetside Fish Ball Sauce

Fish ball is one of the Pinoy's most loved *merienda* and in fact so popular, some Filipinos would refer to it as an "anytime snack." Fishball is one of the processed foods that have become extremely popular in the Philippines because they are extremely affordable and readily available. On their own fish balls can be a little bland and dry, so this improvised sweet, sometimes spicy sauce is really a match made in heaven. This can also be served with squid balls, chicken balls or deep fried quail eggs (*kwek-kwek*)—all popular afternoon snacks on Manila's streets.

¼ cup (60 ml) store bought fermented fish paste (*bagoong balayan*)
¼ cup (60 ml) vinegar or calamansi juice
2–3 red bird's-eye chilies (*siling labuyo*), chopped

1. In a small mixing bowl, combine the *bagoong* and vinegar or calamansi juice and mix well.
2. Bruise the red chilies with the back of your knife for a hint of spicy or chop the chilies for a spicy kick. Add to the mixing bowl and stir.
3. Serve with your favorite grilled fish and boiled vegetables.

**Good for 2 cups (500 ml)**
**Prep time: 5 minutes**
**Cooking time: 15 minutes**

1 cup (250 ml) water
1 cup (250 ml) lemon-lime soda (Sprite/7-Up)
¼ cup (60 ml) soy sauce
1 tablespoon cornstarch
2 teaspoons flour
¼ cup (50 g) brown sugar
¼ cup (40 g) minced onion
1 tablespoon minced garlic
Salt and pepper, to taste

1. In a medium-sized mixing bowl, combine the water, soda, soy sauce, cornstarch, flour and brown sugar. Mix well until everything is dissolved and free of lumps.
2. Transfer to a casserole and cook on medium heat. Stir continuously until the sauce thickens.
3. Add the onion and garlic and simmer on low heat for another 5 minutes. You can also add red chilies for that sweet spicy taste.
4. Transfer to a sauce dish or metallic-lined small paper plates for a more traditional feel of eating your favorite street foods. It can be served with any fried snacks—some good options are fried fish balls, squid balls, or battered deep fried quail eggs (*kwek kwek*).

# APPETIZERS

In the Philippines, serving meals in courses is not usually practiced. The dishes are normally served simultaneously, leaving the diner to try everything according to their individual appetite and preference. Appetizer is most commonly associated with *pulutan*, or foods that are prepared to be eaten with one's hands, typically as snacks served with alcoholic drinks. *Pulutan* literally means "to pick up" and could be translated as "finger food" in English.

Some basic Filipino appetizers or *pulutan* may include nuts, chips from potato, camote, or cassava, or deep-fried puffed pork skin (*chicharon*). These can all be found ready-made and widely available in the Philippines or in the Filipino specialty stores abroad.

Other classic *pulutan* include fried calamari, fried pork and tofu (*tokwa't baboy*), grilled pork belly (*liempo*), fresh or fried spring rolls (*lumpia*), pork barbecue or *sisig*. A number of these can also be served as main courses on their own. While a number of these *pulutan* are simple fried concoctions, my favorite appetizer is Filipino ceviche (*kinilaw*), which showcases the amazing fresh seafood found in the Philippines and some of the key ingredients of Filipino cuisine such as coconut, calamansi, cane vinegar, chili and more.

Filipino *pulutan* also highlights the culinary innovation of Filipino chefs who, over the decades, have integrated imported cooking techniques with available local ingredients to create entirely new dishes. Dynamite is a great example—a fresh long chili is stuffed with texmex beef filling, cheese, then wrapped like a spring roll and deep-fried. Dipped in ranch dressing, it's a remarkable twist of East and West cooking that has come out of the unique culinary crossroads of the Philippines.

# Filipino Texmex Style Spring Rolls Dynamite

Hailing from the Volcanic region of Bicol and with a spiciness to match is "Dynamite", a texmex inspired provincial creation that is bound to impress your guests and please those who love a spicy kick. Dynamite in essence is a stuffed long green chili, wrapped as a spring roll and fried to crispy perfection. The protruding stem of the chili and resulting explosion in one's mouth combine to form the culinary equivalent of a stick of TNT. Try leaving the chili seeds in for a more intense effect (or to surprise your friends!). You can always balance the spiciness by serving with some ranch dressing. Dynamite showcases the more recent North and Central American influences, as well as the creativity of Filipinos in naming their culinary creations. Still not popular across the Philippines, this dish is normally accompanied with cold beer in homes and watering holes of Bicol. It's fast gaining recognition as an exciting, home grown take on the humble spring roll and finding its way on restaurant menus as well.

**Good for 6–8**
**Prep time: 20 minutes**
**Cooking time: 10 minutes**

2 tablespoons cooking oil

3 cloves garlic, minced

1 medium red onion, finely chopped

1 lb (500 g) ground pork or beef

2 tablespoons taco seasoning (you can use any store bought premix, or just combine ½ tablespoon of each: ground cumin, garlic, onion and dried oregano leaves)

½ teaspoon each of salt and pepper

30–40 long green chilies (*siling mahaba*) usually 4 in/10 cm in length

7 oz (200 g) cheddar cheese, sliced into thin strips about 2 in (5 cm) and make sure it's a bit shorter than the chilies

30–40 pieces *lumpia* wrappers, about 6 in/15 cm diameter (ordinary Chinese spring roll wrappers may be substituted)

Cooking oil, for frying

Good quality ranch dressing (store bought is fine), to serve

1. In a shallow skillet, heat 2 tablespoons oil and sauté the garlic and onion until fragrant. Add the ground meat, taco seasoning, salt and pepper. Cook for 10–15 minutes, or until the ground meat is browned and cooked through. Set aside to cool.

2. With a sharp paring knife, cut a ½ in (1 cm) slit horizontally just under the stem of each green chili—be sure not to cut all the way through or remove the top entirely. Connecting to this incision, make another long slit down one side of the chili to create an opening flap sufficient to remove the seeds and stuff the chili. Rinse with cold water and let dry.

3. Take a chili and stuff 1 teaspoon of the taco meat mixture—or as much as will fit—along with a strip of cheese. Close the incision around the stuffed chili.

4. On a flat surface, place a single *lumpia* wrapper and roll the chili as you would an ordinary spring roll, except only close one end of the wrapper, the "stem" end of the chili should be left open to leave the iconic "wick" protruding from the Dynamite. Dab some water on the final part of the wrapper to help seal it as needed.

5. In a skillet, pre-heat some cooking oil to 350°F (180°C) and shallow fry the Dynamite, turning once during cooking for 5–7 minutes or until crisp and golden brown. Using tongs or a slotted spoon, transfer the cooked Dynamite to paper towels to remove excess oil prior to serving.

6. Serve hot with a ranch dressing and a cold glass of beer!

**1** Sauté the onion, garlic and ground pork in a little oil, then add the taco seasoning.

**2** Make an incision in the long green chili to create an opening flap so the seeds can be removed.

**3** Stuff the chili with the seasoned ground pork and a long strip of cheese.

**4** On a single *lumpia* wrapper, fold one side in, place the stuffed chili with the stem hanging over the folded in edge of the wrapper. Roll the *lumpia* wrapper as you would a spring roll, but keep one end open with the stem protruding.

**5** Fry the rolls in hot oil on medium heat until golden brown.

# Chris Urbano's Streetside Calamari
## Calamares

Calamares is a popular Filipino snack served freshly cooked by streetside vendors around Manila as a popular *merienda*, or afternoon tea, for hungry passersby. While calamari is served around the world, what makes Filipino Calamares different is the use of smaller, or even baby squid, with a mixture of both the squid body (whether in rings, or square cut pieces) and the tentacles served together. The preparation is usually a light calamansi based marinade, followed by a dusting of cornstarch. When lightly cooked, the squid is springy, but very light and full of crunch. Dipped in spiced vinegar, Calamares is a favorite *pulutan* (an appetizer eaten with hands) and my personal all-time favorite street food snack.

**Good for 6–8 as appetizer**
**Prep time: 10 minutes**
**Cooking time: 10 minutes**

1 lb (500 g) whole small to medium squid, cleaned and cut into bite-sized 1-in (2.5-cm) square pieces. The tentacles can kept intact, or if using larger squid, this can be cut into two uniform pieces
2 tablespoons calamansi juice (if not available use regular lime juice)
1 teaspoon salt
1 teaspoon pepper
1 cup (120 g) cornstarch
2 tablespoons Filipino Style Spiced Vinegar (page 28), to serve

**1.** Place the squid, calamansi juice, salt and pepper into a glass/non-reactive bowl and marinate for at least 5–10 minutes or longer.
**2.** In another glass/ceramic bowl, place the cornstarch and dust each piece of the squid so it is well coated and feels dry to the touch.
**3.** In a shallow skillet or wok, heat the oil to 350°F (180°C) and fry the Calamares in batches. Do not overcrowd the pan or the squid will get soggy. Remove them just as it takes on a golden color. Use tongs or a slotted spoon to remove the Calamares.
**4.** Place the crispy cooked squid on paper towels to absorb excess oil and serve with the Filipino Style Spiced Vinegar.

# Cheesy Baked Mussels in the Shell
## Baked Tahong

Baked mussels is a dish that took some getting used to for me coming from Australia where the classic preparation is to steam mussels in a wine and herb based broth. Though the visual appeal of cheese bubbling in the mussel shells was hard to forget and it makes for a more interesting texture overall with the addition of bread crumbs—I use crispy panko bread crumbs for this purpose. Although preparing the mussels is a bit of work to clean and open the shells, the filling itself is quite easy and then it's just a matter of baking and watch the cheese turn to golden brown bubbly perfection. Perfect to pair with a glass of white wine (try a pinot grigio or sauvignon blanc) and good company—then finish it with this delicious appetizer—you won't be able to stop at one!

**Good for 6–8**
**Prep time: 20 minutes**
**Cooking time: 15 minutes**

4 lbs (1.5–2 kg) mussels (*tahong*) cleaned with the other half shell removed, washed with water and patted dry

½ cup (125 g) butter, softened

¼ cup (35 g) chopped garlic

½ cup (15 g) finely chopped parsley

1 cup (125 g) grated cheddar cheese

2 teaspoons salt

1 teaspoon ground black pepper

1 cup (125 g) Japanese bread crumbs (*panko*)

1 tablespoon paprika (for topping)

1. Pre-heat the oven to 350°F (180°C).
2. In a medium-sized mixing bowl, mix the butter, garlic, parsley (reserve about 1 tablespoon of parsley for topping later) and cheese. Season with salt and pepper.
3. Spoon about half a teaspoon of the butter mixture into each mussel shell. Sprinkle a pinch of bread crumbs over each mussel for texture.
4. Line them up on a baking tray and bake in the oven for 10–15 minutes until it turns bubbly and golden brown.
5. Transfer to a serving dish and sprinkle the top with paprika and some fresh finely chopped parsley before serving.

# Vegetarian Spring Rolls Lumpiang Togue

The Filipinos' love for spring rolls is evident in the variety of spring rolls available in the country—and it's common in parts of Manila to see food vendors on foot with large *bilaos* on their heads calling out for their everyday *suki* (loyal customers) at *merienda* time. I love Lumpiang Togue as this is a healthier alternative to the common Lumpiang Shanghai, though equally delicious. A hot parcel of fresh bean sprouts, carrots, green beans and tofu, crispy fried exterior and the touch of acid and sour from the vinegar. It's great as either an afternoon snack, or with drinks before the main meal! In the past, I always put spring rolls in the "too hard" category as a home chef, but it's well worth learning once and for all how to roll a spring roll—you'll be surprised how quick and easy it actually is!

**Good for 6–8 as a snack/appetizer**
**Prep time: 40 minutes**
**Cooking time: 15 minutes**

2 tablespoons cooking oil
2 tablespoons minced garlic
¼ cup ( 85 g) finely diced red onion
1 medium carrot, cut into long thin strips (matchsticks)
½ cup (150 g) thinly sliced green (Baguio) beans
1 lb (500 g) bean sprouts (*togue*)
3 pieces (7 oz/200 g) firm tofu, cut into strips and fried
2 tablespoons soy sauce
Salt and pepper, to taste
10–15 pieces large *lumpia* wrapper
Cooking oil, for shallow frying—as needed
Filipino Style Spiced Vinegar (page 28), for dipping

1. In a shallow skillet, heat 2 tablespoons oil and sauté the garlic and onion. Add the carrots and green beans. Throw in the bean sprouts (*togue*) and fried tofu. Season with the soy sauce, salt and pepper.
2. Using a strainer, pour the mixture to remove excess liquid and let it cool. Set aside.
3. On a flat surface, place a single *lumpia* wrapper and put 2–4 tablespoons of the mixture on each wrapper. Fold the ends and roll tightly as you would an ordinary spring roll. It should be larger than a normal spring roll, ideally measuring around 4 inches long and 1 inch wide (10 cm long x 2.5 cm wide). Dab some water on the final part of the wrapper to help seal it as needed.
4. In another skillet, add oil to a depth of about ½ inch (1 cm) and heat to 350°F (180°C). Shallow fry the lumpia in batches for 5–7 minutes or until golden brown, turning once to ensure both sides are well cooked.
5. Serve with the Filipino Style Spiced Vinegar.

# "Shanghai" Spring Rolls Lumpiang Shanghai

Lumpiang Shanghai is the classic Filipino version of the Chinese fried egg rolls or spring rolls. It is very popular during family gatherings and is a main stay party food for large events given it is easy to pass around and eat with your hands. Although it can be a little laborious to prepare many rolls, it makes a great activity for family or friends in anticipation of a celebration—many hands make light work so they say! While the basic recipe contains a combination of ground chicken and pork and finely diced onion and carrot for the filling, I like to elevate the flavors by including mushrooms and jicama (*singkamas*). I love the speckled variety and different texture from these additions. With the meat filling and sweetness from the carrots, Lumpiang Shanghai is normally paired with tomato sauce or sweet chili. The uncooked rolls freeze well, so I usually prepare a double batch and pop half in the freezer for a quick dish on another night.

**Good for 6–8 as snack/appetizer**
**Prep time: 30 minutes**
**Cooking time: 15 minutes**

½ lb (250 g) ground pork
½ lb (250 g) ground chicken
¼ cup (85 g) finely diced green onions (scallions)
¼ cup (85 g) finely diced carrots
2 tablespoons finely diced garlic
¼ cup (85 g) finely diced shiitake mushrooms
¼ cup (85 g) finely diced jicama (*singkamas*)
2 tablespoons sesame oil
2 tablespoons soy sauce
½ tablespoon each of salt and pepper
40–50 pieces small *lumpia* wrappers
Sweet chili sauce or ketchup, to serve (or try my Homemade Ketchup on page 32)
Cooking oil, as required

1. In a large mixing bowl, mix together all the ground meat and finely chopped vegetables. Add the sesame oil, soy sauce, salt, pepper and stir well. You can check the taste by frying a small amount of mixture in a pan and add a little more condiments if required.
2. On a flat surface, place a single *lumpia* wrapper and put 1–2 tablespoons of the mixture on it. Fold the ends and roll tightly as you would an ordinary spring roll. Dab some water on the final part of the *lumpia* wrapper to help seal it as needed.
3. In a shallow skillet, add oil to a depth of about ½ inch (1 cm) and heat to 350°F (180°C). Shallow fry the spring rolls on medium heat for 5–10 minutes or until crisp and golden brown, turning once during cooking to allow both sides to cook.
4. Serve with sweet chili sauce or Homemade Ketchup.

# Crispy Tofu 'N' Pork
## Tokwa't Baboy

Translating literally to Tofu'n'Pork, *Tokwa't Baboy* is a salty/sour snack usually consumed on its own with drinks, or sometimes as an accompaniment for congee (*arroz caldo*). Usually a mix of pork meat, pork ears, or skin are used to give the dish more texture and crunch. I tend to just use pork belly, which is usually easier to find in stores, when making it at home or when I've foreign friends who are averse to eating those parts of the animal. For vegetarians, feel free to forego the pork and focus on the tofu—in this case use a vegetable stock for the sauce instead of pork broth. Whatever you opt for, this is a delicious and truly Pinoy way to get a party starting along with some ice cold Filipino beers.

**Good for 6–8**
**Prep time: 1 hour**
**Cooking time: 15–20 minutes**

½ lb (250 g) pork ears
½ lb (250 g) pork belly
½ cup (80 g) onion, quartered
1 teaspoon whole peppercorns
2 bay leaves
1 tablespoon salt
2 blocks (16 oz/450 g) firm tofu
Cooking oil, as required
2 tablespoons finely sliced green onions
  (scallions) or leeks
2–3 red bird's-eye chilies (*siling labuyo*),
  sliced finely
2–3 long green chilies (*siling mahaba*), sliced
  finely

SAUCE
1 cup (250 ml) vinegar
½ cup (125 ml) soy sauce
¼ cup (60 ml) reserved pork broth (from
  cooking the pork)
1 tablespoon sugar
2 tablespoons finely diced garlic
½ cup (80 g) finely diced white onion

1. Fill a deep pot with water and bring the pork ears and pork belly with the onion, peppercorns, bay leaves and salt to a boil or until the meat becomes tender. Slice the meat into bite-sized pieces and set aside. Reserve ¼ cup (60 ml) of the broth and set aside.
2. Slice the tofu into large cubes. Heat a little oil in a pan and shallow fry them, turning once. Remove the tofu from the pan once they turn golden brown. Place on paper towels to remove excess oil.
3. In the same pan, shallow fry the sliced, boiled pork belly/ears until golden brown and slightly crispy on the outside. Remove and place on paper towels to remove excess oil.
4. To make the Sauce, grab a small saucepan and throw in the vinegar, soy sauce, reserved pork broth, sugar, garlic and onion and bring it to a boil.
5. In a platter, arrange the tofu and pork together. Pour the Sauce on the pork and tofu combo and top it with finely sliced green onions or leeks and chilies for color and a flavor kick. Serve with cold beer and good company.

# Fish Ceviche with Bird's-Eye Chili and Cilantro Kinilaw

*Kinilaw* is the Philippines' answer to ceviche, a seafood dish that has undergone "fireless cooking" where raw seafood is slowly cooked by immersing the meat in a mild form of acid from either citrus fruit or vinegar. While you can turn almost any raw seafood into *kinilaw*, my favorite fish to use is mackerel (*tangigue*) or tuna—both of these can be bought in large, meaty fillets that are easy to slice at home, and taste fantastic semi-raw, or just lightly cooked. The flavors are complex, biting, and fresh. The first time I tried *kinilaw* it completely reset my expectations for what Filipino food could be. Served in a lowball, or martini glass, this could be a much savored tapas or appetizer found in any cosmopolitan capital in the world.

**Good for 10–12 as appetizers**
**Prep time: 25 minutes**
**Cooking time: 15 minutes**

2 lbs (1 kg) mackerel fillets (*tangigue*), skin and bone removed, chopped into ¾-in (2-cm) cubes. Other options include: marlin, milk fish, tuna and sword fish. If fish is unavailable; you can also use oysters, shrimp, or lobster meat. Use only the freshest seafood available and clean it thoroughly.
2 cups (500 ml) vinegar (preferably *tuba* or *sukang Iloko*)
8 shallots, minced
4 tablespoons grated ginger
3 long green chilies (*siling mahaba*), deseeded and thinly sliced
1 tablespoon calamansi zest, grated
1 medium red onion, sliced thinly
2 bell peppers (red and green), sliced into thin strips
¼ cup (60 ml) calamansi juice
1 cup (250 ml) coconut cream
1½ tablespoons salt
1 teaspoon pepper
¼ cup (85 g) chopped coriander leaves (cilantro)
Red bird's-eye chilies (*siling labuyo*), chopped, according to taste

1. In a large mixing bowl, wash the fish cubes with 1 cup (250 ml) of vinegar to remove any fishy smell or slimy residue until the outside surfaces of the fish just turn opaque. Discard the vinegar.
2. In a large glass mixing bowl, combine the fish cubes with the shallots, ginger, green chilies, calamansi zest, onion and bell peppers.
3. Add the remaining 1 cup (250 ml) vinegar, calamansi juice and coconut cream and stir until mixed evenly. Season with salt and pepper. Refrigerate for 15 minutes or until the fish cubes are "cooked" in the vinegar's acidity.
4. Serve in individual martini glasses or arrange on a stylish share platter and garnish with finely chopped flecks of coriander leaves and bird's-eye chili, according to taste.

**NOTE:** Cooked in vinegar and citrus *kinilaw* can be tough to pair with a wine, though it's worth trying with a slightly sweeter and high acid white wine—sauvignon blanc or petit manseng varieties can work well.

# Filipino Crispy Seafood Fritters
## Ukoy

Ukoy originated in Laguna to the south of Manila where there are plenty of lake farmed fish and seafood. It is a savory pancake using baby shrimp or fish and grated starchy vegetables—like sweet potato—as main ingredients. Fried in oil, it's a crispy, salty seafood delight, I can only compare it to the classic combo of "fish and chips"—without the "and". You dip it to a spicy seasoned vinegar so it cuts the oil from the frying, and the sourness of dipping vinegar balances out the slight sweetness of the sweet potato (you can substitute regular potatoes if you prefer it more savory). There are no hard rules for how your *ukoy* should look or what can go in it, though I like to use tiny silverfish (*dulong*, usually found in the freezer section of Asian grocery stores) and I grate the sweet potato (*camote*) quite fine, so mine tend to have a very smooth and consistent texture, compared to the classic version one usually finds in the *carinderias* of Manila. They are quite coarse and crunchy as a result of using baby shrimps with the shells still on.

**Good for 6–8**
**Prep time: 15 minutes**
**Cooking time: 15 minutes**

1½ cups (500 g) grated sweet potato
   (*camote*)
1 egg white
1 tablespoon minced garlic
½ lb (250 g) small shrimp, cleaned and
   trimmed or if available use tiny silverfish
   (*dulong*)
3 tablespoons cornstarch
1 tablespoon cold water
1 teaspoon salt
1 teaspoon pepper
Cooking oil, as required for shallow frying
Filipino Style Spiced Vinegar (page 28), to
   serve

1. In a large mixing bowl, mix the sweet potato, egg white, garlic and shrimp. Set aside.
2. Combine the cornstarch with water, stir and add it to the shrimp mixture. Blend it well and season with salt and pepper. Drain any excess liquid with a strainer.
3. Heat the oil in a skillet. Scoop 1–2 tablespoons of the shrimp mixture into the hot oil on medium heat. Fry in batches until crisp and the sides turn golden brown. Remove from the pan and drain any excess oil on paper towels.
4. Serve hot and crispy with your favorite Filipino Style Spiced Vinegar.

# SOUPS AND SALADS

Soups or *sabaw* are fundamental to Filipino cuisine. They are typically served accompanied with a plate of steaming rice, with the soup spooned over the rice to soften it, or often a small appetizer-sized bowl is served with other dishes on the table. Heartier soups can be a meal on its own, supplemented by starchy vegetables such as potato, sweet potato (*camote*) or bananas. They fill the stomach and keep one warm during cooler, rainy days.

Filipino stew (*sinigang*) is typically sour relying on native souring agents including tamarind (*sampaloc*), bilimbi (*kamias*), calamansi or even green mangoes, papaya or guava for slightly sweeter variants. Seafood, beef or pork can go in *sinigang*, along with a medley of fresh tropical vegetables and chilies can be added for a spicy kick.

*Nilagang Baka* or Beef *bulalo* is a savory boiled beef broth that's cooked over several hours rendering the toughest meat soft and flavorsome and unlocks the flavors of the bones and marrow. Simple in name, this style of soup is a showcase of the bold blending of flavors in Filipino cuisine. To the savory broth is added *saba* bananas, or sweet corn balanced by fresh calamansi juice and fish sauce that creates a perfect harmony of flavor.

In the Philippines, salads are not typically served as appetizers or on their own but rather as side dishes paired to another main dish. For example, *pochero* will normally be paired with a tangy eggplant and tomato *ensalada*. While one can serve fried milk fish with the bitter acidity of an *ampalaya* salad.

I love to whip up Pinoy inspired salads and salsas at home, using ingredients like kale, eggplant, tomatoes, calamansi, local honey and cheese. As with all vegetables its best to work with whatever can be sourced locally and in season and mix and match accordingly!

# Salmon in Sour Broth
## Sinigang Na Isda Sa Kamias At Calamansi

As a seafood exporting country, it would be remiss not to
tell you how to cook Filipino stew (*sinigang*) with seafood.
Citrus loves seafood, so when preparing the dish with fish, I
opt for calamansi as the souring agent. Milder than tamarind,
the addition of bilimbi (*kamias*) if you can get your hands on
any will get the broth to that mouth puckering sourness of
tamarind based soups—though on its own, calamansi delivers a
simple, subtle broth perfect for seafood. Aside from salmon,
you can try this recipe with milkfish (*bangus*), grouper (*lapu-
lapu*) or mackerel (*tanigue*) fillets. The citrusy broth is the
perfect way to cut through the fish oil of the salmon bellies.
Keep this one really light, aside from the fish, just some
daikon radish, and fresh greens is all you need in the soup.

**Good for 6–8**
**Prep time: 10 minutes**
**Cooking time: 30 minutes**

6–8 cups (1.5–2 l) water
½ cup (80 g) onion, quartered
½ cup (80 g) tomatoes, quartered
1 tablespoon pounded ginger
¾ cup (180 ml) calamansi juice
1 cup (160 g) sliced bilimbi (*kamias*)
   (optional)
1 salmon head (optional)
1½ lbs (750 g) salmon bellies (salmon
   fillets may also be used)
1 cup (340 g) sliced daikon radish
   (*labanos*)
1 bundle green beans, cut into 1-in
   (2.5-cm) lengths
¼ cup (60 ml) fish sauce (*patis*)
Salt, to taste
1 bundle mustard leaves or water
   spinach (*kangkong*)
2–3 long green chilies (*siling mahaba*)

1. In a large cooking pot add the
water, onion, tomatoes, ginger,
calamansi juice and bilimbi and
bring to a boil before simmering on
medium heat. If using salmon head,
add it now and let it simmer for
10–15 minutes or until the salmon
head releases its natural oils, or you
can add some fish stock if you have
any handy.
2. Add the remaining fish and
vegetables in the order of their
cooking time starting with radish and
let it simmer for 5 minutes. Follow up
with the green beans and let it cook
for 5 minutes.
3. Season with fish sauce and salt.
Remove the pot from the heat and
add the mustard leaves and long
green chilies, allowing it to cook in
the remaining heat.
4. Serve with steaming white
rice and a side of fish sauce with
calamansi on the side to adjust the
taste based on the diner's preference.

# Pork in Sour Guava Broth Sinigang Na Baboy Sa Bayabas

I've loved eating guava since I first came to Southeast Asia almost twenty years ago as a high school student. Depending on their ripeness, they can be consumed as a sweet or an almost sweet/sour if it's still green—and the latter are a terrific, versatile ingredient to use in cooking. *Sinigang* is a Filipino stew dish with almost limitless variation in the choice of ingredients one can use. While *sinigang* is usually a clear soup, when using guavas (*bayabas*), I like to add taro root (*gabi*), which after extended cooking imparts a starchy thickness to the broth. The slight sweetness of the guava pairs best with pork and I like to use the meaty and finely marbeled cut like pork neck fillets. If you're on a budget, pork shoulder or any cut on bone can be used.

**Good for 6–8**
**Prep time: 10 minutes**
**Cooking time: 1 hour 20 minutes**

1½ lbs (750 g) pork neck or 2 lbs (1 kg) pork ribs, cut into 1–2 in (2.5–5 cm) pieces
½ cup (80 g) onion, quartered
1 cup (170 g) tomatoes, quartered
8–10 medium semi-ripe guavas (or ripe guavas for a sweeter broth), peeled and quartered
6–8 cups (1.4–2 l) water
1 cup (340 g) taro (*gabi*), peeled and quartered
1 bundle string beans, cut into 1-in (2.5-cm) lengths
¼ cup (60 ml) fish sauce (*patis*)
Salt, to taste
1 bundle kangkong leaves and stems

1. In a big pot, combine the pork, onion, tomatoes, guavas and water. Cover with a lid and let it simmer for 1 hour until the pork is fork tender. Check on the pot every once in a while and remove any impurities that float on top to make the broth clear.
2. Once the meat is tender, throw in the vegetables in the order of their cooking time. Start with taro and let it simmer for 10 minutes. Follow up with the string beans and let it cook for 5 minutes. Season with fish sauce and salt until you get the desired taste.
3. Add the kangkong and turn off the heat, slightly blanching the kangkong in the soup's heat.
4. Serve hot with steaming hot rice.

# Clam and Native Corn Chowder

Traditional clam chowder is usually a cream-based soup with lots of root vegetables and fresh clams. In the Philippines, however, clam chowder has come to represent a more minimalist and clear broth. While it is quite light, grated white native corn is used to make it more hearty and thick, along with a slight peppery heat from the chili leaves. If not available, water spinach, or regular spinach can be used but consider adding a little paprika to achieve the same effect. A comparatively light and subtle flavored dish, this is a perfect starter or side dish to serve. It's also surprisingly fast and easy to prepare so a terrific time saver if preparing a lot of dishes.

**Good for 4–6**
**Prep time: 10 minutes**
**Cooking time: 25 minutes**

1 lb (500 g) fresh clams (*halaan*)
2 tablespoons cooking oil
1 tablespoon chopped garlic
¼ cup (40 g) chopped onion
1 tablespoon thinly sliced ginger
1 cup (180 g) grated native corn
1 native corn, chopped into 6 thin slices
6 cups (1.5 l) water
¼ cup (60 ml) fish sauce (*patis*)
Salt and pepper, to taste
1 cup (80 g) chili leaves or spinach

1. Clean and brush the clam shells under running water. Make sure to remove any moss and hair around it. Let it sit in a basin of water for 20 minutes until it spits out any remaining sand inside the shell.
2. In a large pot, heat the oil and sauté the garlic, onion and ginger on medium heat. Add the corn and clams and simmer for 5 minutes.
3. Pour in the water and let it simmer for 5–10 minutes or until the clams open and the corn is tender.
4. Season with fish sauce, salt and pepper until you get your desired taste.
5. Add the chili leaves and let it simmer for a further two minutes until the leaves have wilted.
6. Serve while steaming hot.

# Seaweed Salad Medley Ensaladang Lato

*Lato* is a variety of edible seaweed that can be eaten raw. It is shaped like tiny green grapes and tastes literally like the sea when they burst in your mouth. *Guso* on the other hand is woody-looking and crunchy but they taste the same. These are both widely available in the Philippines, but of course you should use whatever type of fresh edible seaweed available where you live, the rest of the ingredients are quite easy to find. Once you've sourced your ingredients, it's just a case of tossing this salad together and serving—ideally with fried, or grilled seafood—what grows together goes together as they say!

**Good for 6–8**
**Prep time: 10 minutes**
**Cooking time: none**

2 cups (200 g) fresh *lato* seaweed
2 cups (200 g) fresh *guso* seaweed
½ cup (80 g) thinly sliced onion
1 cup (200 g) thinly sliced tomatoes
1 cup (200 g) green mango, cut into strips
¼ cup (40 g) chopped green onions (scallions)
Half a salted egg, to serve

### DRESSING
3 tablespoons spiced vinegar
¼ cup (60 ml) calamansi juice
3 tablespoons fish sauce (*patis*)
1 teaspoon pepper

**1.** Clean the seaweeds under running water to remove any sand and dirt.
**2.** In a large mixing bowl, combine the seaweeds, onion, tomatoes, green mango and green onions. Set aside and chill in the fridge for 10–20 minutes.
**3.** Make the Dressing in a small mixing bowl. Combine the vinegar, calamansi juice, fish sauce and pepper.
**4.** Take out the chilled seaweeds and pour the Dressing. Toss to incorporate all flavors well. Best served with grilled or fried fish, half a salted egg and steaming rice.

# Hearty Bone Marrow Soup

## Bulalo

*Bulalo* is a popular variation of the Nilaga-style soup; it's served in cooler weather and higher altitudes—and the most famous dish in Tagaytay, a cooler mountainous town, about two hours south of Manila. Two things that make *bulalo* unique are first, that it is slow cooked and uses exclusively the beef shank for the meat. It's very important the bone marrow is included as this adds creamy richness that is iconic of this dish. The second thing is that the dish gets its sweetness from sweet corn, which grows well in and around Tagaytay, so some whole pieces of sweetcorn floating in the bowl is a must when cooking *bulalo*. Best eaten on a wet and windy day—this is guaranteed to warm the body and the heart.

**Good for 6–8**
**Prep time: 15 minutes**
**Cooking time: 2–4 hours**

2 lbs (1 kg) beef shanks, including bone marrow
1 medium (5 oz/150 g) brown onion, sliced into rings
1 teaspoon salt
1 tablespoon whole black peppercorns
10–12 cups (2.5 l) water
2 medium potatoes (10 oz/300 g), slice into six or eight pieces
2 pieces sweet corn, cut into rounds about 1-in (2.5-cm) thick
½ head cabbage, cut into quarters
1 cup (150 g) string beans, cut into 2-in (5-cm) lengths
2 small bundles *pechay* (can use bok choy, or any other similar Asian green leaf vegetable)
¼ cup (60 ml) fish sauce (*patis*), to serve
1 tablespoon calamansi or regular lime juice, to serve

1. In a large cooking pot, add the raw beef, onion, salt, peppercorns and water.
2. Bring to a boil and let simmer, under a pot cover, for 2–4 hours until the meat is very tender/falling off the bone. While simmering, skim off any impurities that rise to the surface for a clearer broth.
3. Season the broth with a little fish sauce and salt, tasting the broth to ensure the right level of salt/savoriness is achieved.
4. Add the potatoes and sweet corn and simmer for a further 10–15 minutes.
5. Once the potatoes are tender, add the remaining vegetables in the order of their cooking time, starting with the cabbage and beans. The *pechay* can be thrown in last, just before serving so it's just lightly blanched.
6. Serve while the broth is hot, with steaming white rice and a small sauce dish containing fish sauce and calamansi or lime juice that can be added to the soup according to individual preference.

# Sour & Bitter Beef Stew
## Papaitan

*Papaitan* is not for the culinary faint-hearted, though this dish is worth a try if you want to experience one of the rarest combinations—a dish that is both sour and bitter at the same time. Originating in the Ilocos province, *papaitan* uses goat innards such as lungs, kidneys, tripe, intestines, liver, pancreas, and bile, which makes it bitter. While I've presented the classic recipe below, it's possible to use goat or beef, with or without the bile, depending on your preference. I'm not a huge fan of innards in cooking, though in Southeast Asia, nothing goes to waste! A good option if you prefer the flavor and texture of regular cuts of meat is to prepare this predominantly using those, along with some kidney or tripe to get some of the effect.

**Good for 6–8**
**Prep time: 40 minutes**
**Cooking time: 25 minutes**

2 lbs (1 kg) beef or goat innards (any combination of lungs, kidneys, tripe, intestines, liver and pancreas—you can also add beef, like chuck steak or spare ribs)
½ cup (120 g) sliced calamansi limes
¼ cup (60 g) sliced ginger
2 tablespoons salt
2 tablespoons cooking oil, as required
½ cup (80 g) chopped onion
2 tablespoons minced garlic
¼ cup (40 g) sliced ginger
8 cups (2 l) water
7 oz (200 g) whole unripe tamarind pods (or 1 tablespoon of tamarind powder can be substituted)
2 cups (500 ml) water for boiling tamarind pods
¼ cup (60 ml) bile (if not available, try using *malunggay* leaves, bay leaves, or bitter gourd)
5 red bird's-eye chilies (*siling labuyo*), sliced
1 cup (100 g) tamarind leaves
¼ cup (60 ml) fish sauce (*patis*)
Salt and pepper, to taste

1. In a large pot filled with water, boil together the innards, calamansi limes, ginger and salt. Let it simmer for 10–15 minutes to clean the innards from impurities. Once done, wash it in running water and chop the innards into bite-sized pieces.
2. In another large pot, heat the oil and sauté the onion, garlic and ginger until fragrant on medium heat. Add the innards and sauté for 5 minutes to allow the flavors to combine.
3. Boil tamarind pods in 2 cups of water for 20–30 mins until soft. Pour through a strainer, and use a potato masher to press the pulp in the strainer to extract as much tamarind liquid as possible. Set aside. If using tamarind powder, you can skip this step.
4. Pour 8 cups of water to the pot with the innards and let it boil for 1–2 hours on high heat or until the innards are fork tender. You can also use a pressure cooker to cook the innards faster.
5. Once fork tender, add the bile 1 teaspoon at a time and adjust the bitterness according to your taste.
6. Add the tamarind leaves and tamarind liquid or tamarind powder. Season with fish sauce, salt and pepper. Adjust the flavors according to your taste preference.
7. Serve while still hot and best served with beer.

# Beef Soup with Plantain Nilagang Baka

*Nilagang baka* sounds plain, but it occupies a special place in the heart of Filipinos as one of those heartwarming dishes. While simple on the surface this dish actually weaves many flavors into a single, steaming bowl. More a method of cooking, than a specific recipe, *nilaga* (literally boiled) can be prepared using beef or pork and contain a wide range of vegetables. Typically whatever is available fresh locally goes into the pot. Importantly though, some vegetables should add bitterness (such as *pechay*) while others are sweeter (such as plaintain banana or sweet potato). It's important to have a balance of both. When served with fish sauce (*patis*) and calamansi juice this humble beef broth soup is elevated to a perfect balance of salty, sweet, sour, bitter and savoriness—and the ability to mix and match vegetables to whatever is available locally makes this a mainstay recipe across the Philippines. In my *nilaga* I like to use a combination of beef ribs, to enhance the flavor of the beef broth and brisket, which is a rich, meaty cut that rewards slow cooking. I like mine a little more peppery and *nilaga* is not complete for me without plantain bananas, cooked whole with skins on—there is something quite remarkable about a savory soup with bananas added.

**Good for 6–8**
**Prep time: 15 minutes**
**Cooking time: 2–4 hours**

1 lb (500 g) beef short ribs (you can substitute other beef on bone cuts)
1 lb (500 g) beef brisket—cut into 1–2 in (2.5–5 cm) pieces (or can substitute other beef like rump, or flank)
1 medium (5 oz/150 g) brown onion, sliced into rings
1 teaspoon salt
1 tablespoon whole black peppercorns
10–12 cups (2.5 l) water
2 medium (10 oz/300 g) potatoes, slice into six or eight pieces
4–6 pieces plantain bananas (can use other bananas but consider using less/smaller pieces if it is a sweet banana)
1 cup (150 g) green beans, cut into 2-in (5-cm) lengths
½ head cabbage, cut into four to six wedges
2 small bundles *pechay* (can use bok choy, or any other similar Asian green leafy vegetables)
¼ cup (60 ml) fish sauce (*patis*), to serve
1 tablespoon calamansi or regular lime juice, to serve

**1.** In a large cooking pot, add the beef, onion, salt, peppercorns and water.
**2.** Bring to a boil and let simmer for 2–4 hours until the meat is very tender/falling off the bone. The exact time will depend on the cuts of meat you're using. While simmering, skim off any impurities that rise to the surface for a clearer broth.
**3.** Season the broth with a little fish sauce and salt, tasting the broth to ensure the right level of salt/savoriness is achieved.
**4.** Add the potatoes and whole plantain bananas and simmer for a further 10–15 minutes.
**5.** Once the potatoes are tender, add the remaining vegetables in the order of their cooking time, starting with the cabbage and beans. The *pechay* can be thrown in last right before serving so it's just lightly blanched.
**6.** Serve while the broth is hot, with steaming white rice and small sauce dishes containing fish sauce and calamansi or lime juice that can be added to the soup according to individual preference.

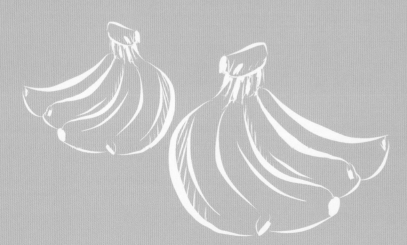

# Tamarind Beef Soup Sinigang Na Baka

Showcasing the versatility of Filipino stew (*sinigang*), here's a very different take on this household favorite. Tamarind or *sampalok* is considered the "classic" souring agent used in preparing *sinigang* in the Philippines. It might be because of my love for Malay *rendang*, where the beef is marinated in tamarind as part of the preparation but I love to use beef in *sinigang* with a tamarind broth. I also like it spicy! The sour/ spicy taste needs getting used to, but it's quite easy to get hooked. In addition to doubling the recommended amount of chilies in the dish, I'll ensure to fish out one or two whole ones and make sure they end up on my plate. I normally cook this earlier in the day, so often opt for beef rib, or even shank which I slow cook till it's falling from the bone, though if you have less time beef chuck is a good choice.

**Good for 6–8**
**Prep time: 10 minutes**
**Cooking time: 2 hours 20 minutes**

2 lbs (1 kg) beef chuck, cut into cubes
½ cup (80 g) onion, quartered
½ cup (100 g) tomatoes, quartered
10–12 cups (2.5 l) water
2 cups (400 g) of fresh tamarind pods (*sampalok*) or substitute equivalent of tamarind powder
2 cups (500 ml) water for boiling tamarind pods
1 cup (300 g) daikon radish (*labanos*)
1 cup (250 g) eggplant (*talong*), sliced diagonally
1 bundle green beans, cut into 2-in (5-cm) lengths
3–6 long green chilies (*siling mahaba*)
¼ cup (60 ml) fish sauce (*patis*)
Salt, to taste
1 bunch *pechay* leaves

1. In a large cooking pot add the beef, onion, tomatoes and water. Cover and let it simmer for 2 hours until the beef is fork tender. Check on the pot every once in a while and remove any impurities that float on top to make the broth clear.
2. In another small pot, put some water and boil the tamarind pods for 30 minutes. Mash the tamarind with a potato masher to release the juice. Pour through a strainer to remove the seeds and shell fragments of the tamarind and set the liquid aside.
3. Once the meat is tender, add the vegetables in the order of their cooking time. Start by adding the radish and eggplant and let it simmer for 5 minutes. Next, add the green beans and green chilies and let it cook for a further 5 minutes.
4. Add the tamarind juice to the pot and season with fish sauce and salt until you get your desired taste.
5. Turn off the heat and add the *pechay*. Cover with the pot lid and let it cook in the remaining heat until just wilted.
6. Serve in a bowl while still hot, accompanied by steaming hot rice.

# Bitter Gourd Salad Ensaladang Ampalaya

This was one of the very first things I made on *Maputing Cooking* when I was starting to explore some of the unique flavors of Philippine vegetables. I've seen bitter gourd (*ampalaya*) before in Australia, but it always looked strange and alien even among the Asian vegetable section. It requires preparation; the key is to salt it first, and as it sweats, the bitterness is reduced down to a more palatable level. This is a really simple preparation that places the *ampalaya* as the hero ingredient, the use of fresh tomatoes, and onion adds complexity. *Bagoong* or *patis* in the dressing adds salt, while sourness comes from the cane vinegar and citrus. Best served alongside crispy fried fish!

**Good for 6–8**
**Prep time: 15 minutes**
**Cooking time: No cooking needed**

2 pieces medium sized bitter gourd (*ampalaya*), sliced thinly
½ cup (100 g) rock salt
1 tablespoon *bagoong*, optional
3–4 pieces medium-size native or salad tomato
½ onion, sliced thinly (red onions or onion leeks may be substituted for a milder taste)

**DRESSING**
¼ cup (60 ml) cane vinegar (calamansi, lemon or lime juice may be substituted)
2 tablespoons fish sauce (*patis*), not required if *bagoong* is used
2 teaspoons sugar (optional)
Ground black pepper, to taste

1. In a large mixing bowl, combine the sliced *ampalaya* with salt and ensure all pieces are well coated. Let it sit for at least 20 minutes and then wash the *ampalaya* thoroughly and set aside.
2. Make the Dressing by combining all the ingredients in a bowl.
3. In a salad bowl, mix the *ampalaya* together with the *bagoong*, Dressing and the tomato and onion—or these can be place on top for visual effect. Chill for 5 minutes before serving.
4. Best served with Crispy Fried Marinated Milk Fish (page 91) and other fried fish or pork to counterbalance the oil from fried foods.

# Filipino Style Calamansi Slaw

In the heat of Australia, coleslaw salads are a favorite at picnics or outdoor barbeques. Usually served chilled, they are a refreshing accompaniment to grilled meats straight off the "barbie". Although the classic coleslaw preparations use mayonnaise, increasingly healthy conscious Australians are going for slaws containing citrus juice and minimal olive oil instead—and letting the freshness of the vegetables do the talking. As a "foreign-noy" I often wish there were more fresh vegetables on the table to complement grilled meats like grilled pork belly (*liempo*) or pork chops. So this recipe is my attempt at creating something light, healthy, but still showcasing Filipino flavors through the calamansi vinaigrette. While I've specified the recipe for cabbage and carrots—which are widely available in the Philippines all year round and have good shelf life—consider adding daikon radish (*labanos*), native cucumbers (*pepino*) or a little watercress to take this slaw to the next level.

**Good for 6–8**
**Prep time: 20 minutes**
**Cooking time: No cooking required**

2 cups (300 g) cabbage, shredded thinly
1 cup (120 g) grated carrots
1 cup (100 g) green onions (scallions) or leeks, sliced diagonally
½ cup (50 g) chopped coriander leaves (cilantro)

**DRESSING**
¼ cup (60 ml) calamansi juice
2 tablespoons cane vinegar
¼ cup (60 ml) olive oil
Salt and pepper, to taste

1. Make the Dressing. In a large mixing bowl, mix together the calamansi juice, vinegar and olive oil to make an emulsion of flavors. Season with salt and pepper and set aside.
2. In a bigger bowl, combine the shredded cabbage, carrots, green onions and coriander leaves.
3. Pour in the Dressing and toss to distribute the flavors evenly. Chill for 10 minutes and serve. Best served with pork chops.

# NOODLES AND PASTAS

Noodles are quick to prepare and can feed the whole *barangay*—so it's no surprise they're a popular choice on Filipino banquet tables—especially celebrations and birthdays where they are eaten as a symbol of longevity. From the translucent, thin vermicelli to thicker round *lomi*, Filipino noodles are typically stir-fried with vegetables or meat like the classic *pancit*, or used in soups like Chicken Sotanghon or beef *pares*.

Noodle dishes in the Philippines tend to reflect their Chinese culinary heritage, but with local and regional variations. Probably the best well known is Pansit Canton a combination of chicken, pork, seafood and stir-fried vegetables. Pansit palabok uses only shrimp and hard boiled eggs as the protein and is colored a bright orange color using *atsuete* or annatto seeds. Pancit Bihon, is a simpler chicken and vegetable stir-fry using the noodles of the same name.

During the 20th century, pasta was introduced to the Philippines through the American culinary influence. However the style of pasta introduced could be considered as "Italian-American" and were cooked using ready-made spaghetti sauce and processed meats like sliced hot dogs. As such Filipino pastas tend to be sweeter and rely on readily available canned goods.

In the Philippines, I like to experiment with different types of *longganisa* when cooking pasta: my favorite is a garlicky *Calumpit longganisa* and Black Bean Rigatoni, which is divine especially when served with the large leafed Philippine oregano and a glass of red wine. Another really interesting combination is to incorporate some of the delicious dried, or smoked seafood into Italian style pastas—dried anchovies (*dilis*) or smoked fish (*tinapa*) work very well as the flavor backbone for simple red sauce pastas. Once you experiment a bit with dishes like these you'll find it very hard to stop!

# Seafood "Malabon" Noodles
## Pancit Malabon

Pancit Malabon is a traditional Filipino dish usually served at a feast or special occasion—especially on birthdays where the use of long egg noodles symbolises longevity and good luck. Annatto seeds are used to color and flavor the dish giving it its distinct bright orange color. Unlike other Filipino noodle dishes, Pancit Malabon predominantly uses seafood as the protein with a distinct shrimp flavor in the sauce. Some chefs like to add other meats like pork or chicken, but I prefer to keep my Pancit Malabon focused on seafood only with the eggs of course—it's also much faster to cook! It can be topped off with a little smoked fish (*tinapa*) or crunchy *chicaron* bits for texture and some concentrated salty flavor.

**Good for 6–8**
**Prep time: 15 minute**
**Cooking time: 60 minutes**

15–20 medium shrimp, heads and shells removed
2 pieces (10 oz/300 g) medium squid, cleaned and sliced in rings (optional)
2 cups (500 ml) water
½ cup (120 g) carrot, cut into long thin strips (matchsticks)
½ cup (50 g) chopped celery stick
1 medium brown onion, thinly sliced
10–15 whole black peppercorns
10 oz (300 g) Malabon noodles (or any thick, round rice noodle)
Cooking oil, as required
2 cups (500 ml) reserved shrimp stock
2 tablespoons fish sauce (*patis*)
Salt and pepper, to taste
6 tablespoons all-purpose flour
2 cups (300 g) chopped Napa (Chinese) cabbage
½ cup (50 g) smoked fish (*tinapa*) flakes
½ cup (50 g) chopped green onions (scallions)
3 hard boiled eggs, sliced

### ANNATTO WATER
2 tablespoons annatto seeds
2 cups (500 ml) water

1. Prepare the Annatto Water by boiling the annatto seeds in 2 cups of water for 5 minutes. Strain and set aside.
2. Remove the head and shells from the shrimp. Set the shrimp meat aside. Put the head and shells with 2 cups water in a saucepan, along with a little carrot, celery, onion and whole peppercorns for 20 minutes to create an improvised shrimp stock. Sieve and set the shrimp stock aside.
3. Soak the noodles in a bowl of water until it gets soft. Drain the water. Bring a large saucepan of water to a boil. Quickly submerge the noodles and cook for 2–3 minutes or until soft. Drain the water and set the noodles aside.
4. Heat some oil in a deep skillet, quickly pan-fry the shrimp for around 30 seconds per side or until just cooked. Remove the shrimp and set aside. In the same skillet, quickly pan-fry the squid (if using) for 1–2 minutes until just cooked.
5. Add the reserved shrimp stock, Annatto Water and fish sauce to the same skillet. Bring to a boil then reduce to low heat and simmer. Add the flour, 1 tablespoon at a time, stirring through until a thick rich consistency is reached.
6. Add the Napa cabbage and simmer for a further 1–2 minutes.
7. Arrange the noodles on a serving platter and pour over the sauce with the cooked cabbage. Add the cooked shrimp (if using). Toss the noodles until the sauce is well distributed.
8. Top with *tinapa* flakes, chopped green onions and sliced oiled egg.

# Black Bean and Longganisa Sausage Rigatoni

This recipe is one of my first culinary experiments on my show *Maputing Cooking.* I really love cooking pastas, they're quick, easy to do at home and make for great leftovers—how much better if I could incorporate traditional Filipino flavors to the mix! *Longganisa* is the name given to local Filipino sausage that resembles and was inspired by Spanish *charcuterie* like *chorizo*. Of course every region of the Philippines now has its own take on *longganisa*, from the very sweet (such as that from Cebu or Pampanga) to more savory (like Vigan or Tuguegarao). But my favorite comes from Calumpit in Bulacan province just North of Metro Manila. Calumpit *longganisa* is garlicky—very garlicky. So you don't need to add garlic to this recipe. While you can try it with any pasta I go with rigatoni, a fairly large elongated hollow tube of pasta. The inside is large enough to catch the fermented black soybeans and bits of *longganisa* when the sauce is stirred through!

**Good for 4–5**
**Prep time: 15 mins**
**Cooking time: 25 mins**

2 cups (500 ml) water
10 pieces *longganisa*, peeled and cut into chunks (Calumpit, or any salty/garlicky *longganisa*, *chorizo* may be substituted)
Olive oil, as required to sauté
1 medium-sized white onion, cut thinly
1 large red bell pepper, cut into long thin strips (matchsticks)
6–8 fresh Cuban oregano (also known as Mexican mint, or Indian borage), sliced into thin strips
1 cup (250 ml) red wine (ideally a lighter style wine such as pinot noir)
½ cup (80 g) fermented black soybeans (*taosi*), soaked in water for 20 mins
2 cups (300 g) cherry tomatoes, sliced in half
Salt and pepper, to taste
10 oz (300 g) rigatoni pasta

1. In a shallow skillet, pour the of water and boil the *longganisa* until it turns dark brown. Once cooked, remove the skin and strings and cut it into little chunks.
2. In a separate skillet, heat some olive oil and sauté the onion and bell pepper on medium heat. Add the *longganisa* and the oregano leaves and let it simmer for 5 minutes.
3. Add the red wine and allow it to simmer for 3–5 mins or until reduced.
4. Add the tomatoes and fermented black soybeans mix well and simmer on low heat for 10–15 mins until the tomatoes soften and break up. Season with salt and pepper, to taste.
5. Boil some water in a large pot and cook the pasta according to instructions, for about 10–12 minutes or until al dente. Drain the pasta using a strainer.
6. Transfer the pasta to the skillet with the sauce and mx well. Serve with red wine.

# Hearty Beef Noodle Soup Beef Pares Mami

I used to enjoy rich beef *pares* on the streetsides of Metro Manila when I was a college student. It's a simple, thick, heartwarming and nourishing beef soup. It's often served in a small cup—a great snack, or *merienda*, but often not a full meal on its own. Beef *mami* on the other hand, is more complete, but I find the broth a little bland—so what better way than to combine the two!

**Good for 6–8**
**Prep time: 15 minutes**
**Cooking time: 2 hours**

1 lb (500 g) beef brisket
Cooking oil, as required
4 tablespoons chopped garlic
1-in (2.5-cm) piece ginger
1 medium onion, chopped
4 cups (1 l) reserved beef stock
4 cups (1 l) water
¼ cup (60 ml) soy sauce
¼ cup (50 g) brown sugar
5 pieces star anise
10 oz (300 g) round fresh *miki* noodles (any dried egg noodles can be used)
2 cups (300 g) Napa (Chinese) cabbage
4 hard boiled eggs, sliced
½ cup (50 g) chopped green onions (scallions)
2 tablespoons fish sauce (*patis*) for serving
Salt and ground black pepper, to taste

1. Fill a large pot, or pressure cooker, with water. Add the beef brisket and bring to a boil. Allow about two hours for conventional cooking or 20–30 minutes in a pressure cooker—it's a good idea to put this to slow cook earlier in the day.
2. Remove the tender brisket and reserve the water it was cooked for use as a beef stock.
3. In another saucepan, toast about 3 tablespoons of chopped garlic in some cooking oil. Set aside.
4. In the same saucepan, sauté the remaining garlic, ginger and medium onion until cooked.
5. Roughly chop the brisket and add to the saucepan and sauté for 2–3 minutes.
6. Add 4 cups of the reserved beef stock, 4 cups of water, soy sauce, brown sugar and star anise, bring to a boil and then simmer for 10–15 mins until the soup begins to reduce.
7. Return the soup to a boil and add the egg noodles and Napa cabbage. Cook for 2–3 minutes or until the noodles are soft.
8. Serve in bowls topped with slices of hard boiled egg, chopped green onions and toasted garlic. Fish sauce, salt and pepper can be added at the table according to taste!

# Chicken Noodle Soup Chicken Sotanghon

Chicken Sotanghon is a delicious chicken noodle soup that is popular as a comfort food, or when feeling a bit under the weather. What makes this dish different is the use of the glass noodles (so*tanghon*), and the use of annatto seeds (*atsuete*) which impart the unique orange color to the broth. Known as the "poor man's saffron", annatto seeds originated in Central America, and is also common in Mexican and Caribbean cooking. So the use of annatto in a chicken noodle soup is another example of culinary fusion in the Philippines between Spanish/Mexican and Chinese culinary influences. Annatto seeds are available at most Asian grocery stores.

1. Boil the chicken breast in 1L water for 20–30 mins until cooked through and tender. Reserve the cooking liquid.
2. Prepare the Annatto Water by combining 2 tablespoons of annatto seeds in 1 cup of water in a small saucepan. Boil for 5 minutes or until the water changes to an orange color. Strain the annatto-infused water through a strainer and set aside.
3. In a deep pot, heat the oil and sauté the garlic and onion on medium heat until fragrant. Add the chicken breast, carrots and mushrooms. Toss and cook for 3–5 minutes for the flavors to develop.
4. Pour in the chicken stock and water and let it boil for 10 minutes.
5. Add the Annatto Water and glass noodles. Season with fish sauce, salt and pepper and let it simmer for 10 more minutes before turning off the heat.
6. Garnish with green onions and sliced hard boiled egg before serving.

**Good for 6–8**
**Prep time: 10 minutes**
**Cooking time: 20 minutes**

1 lb (500 g) chicken breast, boiled and
   torn into strips
¼ cup (60 ml) cooking oil
2 tablespoons chopped garlic
½ cup (80 g) chopped onion
½ cup (120 g) carrots, cut into long thin
   strips (matchsticks)
½ cup (60 g) sliced wood-ear mushroom,
   (other types of mushrooms may be
   substituted)
3 cups (750 ml) chicken stock (from
   boiling the chicken breast)
3 cups (750 ml) water
7 oz (200 g) glass noodles (so*tanghon*)
¼ cup (60 ml) fish sauce (*patis*)
Salt and pepper, to taste
¼ cup (15 g) chopped green onions
   (scallions)
2–3 hard boiled eggs, sliced into four
   equal parts

**ANNATTO WATER**
2 tablespoons annatto seeds
1 cup (250 ml) water

# Smoked Fish and Fresh Tomato Fettucine Tinapasta

Tinapasta is what you get when you mix smoked fish (*tinapa*) with pasta! I can't claim to be the first person in the Philippines experimenting using local fish in typically oil based or red sauce pastas, though I arrived at this puzzle from a slightly different angle—I was looking for Filipino inspired seafood dishes which I could pair with wine. I love the challenge of pairing red wine with seafood, which bucks conventional wine-pairing wisdom. Philippine anchovies (*dilis*) or *tinapa*, with its smoky characteristics are both perfect options in a tomato or oil based pasta with a glass of sangiovese or tempranillo. As with any pasta, fresh herbs is the key—basil and oregano are extremely easy to grow in pots at home and are the best garnish for this dish.

**Good for 3–4**
**Prep time: 10 minutes**
**Cooking time: 20 minutes**

2 tablespoons olive oil
2 tablespoons chopped garlic
¼ cup (40 g) chopped onion
2 cups (300 g) chopped tomatoes
1 cup (150 g) smoked fish (*tinapa*) flakes, *bangus* or *galunggong*
3 tablespoons lemon juice
10 oz (300 g) fettucine pasta (linguine or spaghetti are good substitutes)
⅓ cup (10 g) sliced black olives
¼ cup (10 g) coarsely chopped basil leaves
¼ cup (15 g) coarsely chopped oregano leaves
Salt and pepper, to taste
Parmesan cheese, to garnish
Chili flakes, to garnish (optional)

1. In a shallow skillet, heat the olive oil and sauté the garlic and onion on medium heat for 3–5 minutes or until fragrant. Add the tomatoes and cook until they're softened, mash them a bit to release their flavor.
2. Throw in the *tinapa* flakes and lemon juice.
3. Prepare the pasta and cook according to instructions until al dente. Strain the pasta and toss it in the *tinapa* sauce. Mix them together to fully coat the pasta with the sauce. Toss the olives, basil and oregano, mix to infuse all flavors together. Adjust the taste by seasoning with salt and pepper.
4. Top with grated parmesan cheese and chili flakes for added spice and kick. Serve and enjoy!

# Taro Leaf Pesto Linguine Laing Linguine

Here's a recipe I learned from Eduardo, a Filipino who lived for a long time in Australia. The dish was innovated out of necessity: "I wanted to make *laing*... but we ran out of rice. The supermarket was closed, and all I had was a pack of linguine. I remembered one of my Aussie friend's favorite things to eat is pesto pasta..." And so the idea of a *laing*-inspired Pesto Linguine was born. This is a really cool East meets West fusion dish. While the taro (*gabi*) offers more bitterness, the use of pili nuts offsets this with additional sweetness. The coconut milk base is creamier than an olive oil-based pesto, but the thickness is cut with the citrus lemon juice.

**Good for 4–6**
**Prep time: 15 minutes**
**Cooking time: 30 minutes**

¼ cup (60 ml) olive oil
10 oz (300 g) medium shrimp, peeled
4 cloves garlic, finely diced
1 teaspoon crushed fresh ginger
4–6 anchovy fillets, in oil
10 oz (300 g) dried taro leaves (*dahon ng gabi*)
3 cups (750 ml) coconut cream
½ cup (100 g) pili nuts
1 lemon, juiced, and peel grated for lemon zest
¼ cup (50 g) parmesan cheese, grated
10 oz (300 g) linguine pasta
4 oz (100 g) *kesong puti* (optional)
2 teaspoons chili flakes, plus more for garnish
Basil leaves, to garnish

**1.** Heat 1 tablespoon of olive oil in a skillet and fry the shrimp on high heat for 2 minutes each side or until just cooked. Remove and set aside.
**2.** In the same pan, sauté the garlic, ginger and anchovies on medium heat. Throw in the taro leaves. Add 1 cup of the coconut cream and simmer for 5 mins. Add another cup of coconut cream and simmer for another 10–15 minutes on low heat until the leaves are soft and pulling apart. Set aside to cool down.
**3.** In a food processor, or using a suitable container and an immersion or stick blender, combine the cooked taro leaves, pili nuts, 1 teaspoon lemon zest, ¼ cup lemon juice, remaining olive oil and parmesan cheese and blend on moderate setting until well-combined.
**4.** In a large pot, bring some salted water to a boil and cook the linguine for 10–12 minutes or until al dente. Drain with a strainer. Set aside.
**5.** Return the cooked pasta to the pot and add the taro pesto, shrimp, another cup of coconut cream, another tablespoon of olive oil and 2 teaspoons of chili flakes. Toss until the pasta is completely covered with the sauce. Simmer for another 2–3 minutes or until the sauce coats all the pasta.
**6.** Transfer to a plate and garnish with *kesong puti* and sprinkling of chili flakes and some fresh basil if you have any handy.

# Stir-Fried Egg Noodles with Pork Pancit Canton Guisado

Here's another variety of noodles (*pancit*) that is quick and easy to try at home—Pancit Canton Guisado. A dry stir-fry noodle, using pork, sausages and a medley of vegetables. It's simple to prepare, fast to cook and delicious to eat. While fresh noodles are superior, with this dish, I'm going for convenience, so I'll open two packs of instant noodles from the pantry (though I often throw away the flavor enhancer packets in favor of my own flavor enhancements!) You can even overload this with vegetables and it becomes a real "power bowl" of nutrients. This is a perfect way to refuel quickly after a good workout or an active day.

**Good for 6–8**
**Prep time: 10 minutes**
**Cooking time: 20 minutes**

3 cloves garlic, minced
1 medium onion, sliced
Cooking oil, as required
10 oz (300 g) pork, sliced thinly
1 Chinese sausage, sliced diagonally (optional)
½ cup (50 g) green beans, sliced diagonally
½ cup (120 g) carrot, cut into long thin strips (matchsticks)
½ cup (50 g) chopped celery stick
½ cup (75 g) thinly sliced cabbage
1 teaspoon fish sauce (*patis*)
3 tablespoons soy sauce
Salt and pepper, to taste
2–3 cups (500–750 ml) chicken stock
10 oz (300 g) of fresh egg noodles (or 2 packets of instant noodles)
Calamansi limes, to serve

1. In a wok, or deep skillet, sauté the garlic and onion in a little cooking oil until fragrant.
2. Add the sliced pork and stir fry for 5–6 minutes or until cooked through. Add the sliced Chinese sausage, if using, let it sweat and continue cooking for 2 minutes.
3. Add the green beans, carrot, celery and cabbage in order of their cooking time, stir-frying at the same time.
4. Add the fish sauce, soy sauce and some salt and pepper to taste and stir fry for another minute or two—be careful not to overcook the vegetables. Remove from heat and set aside.
5. In another saucepan, bring 3 cups of chicken stock to a boil. I normally use an organic, chicken stock powder for this, but in a pinch you can use the ones from the instant noodles. Set aside.
6. Boil some water in a large spot and cook the noodles for 2–3 minutes or until softened. Drain the noodles.
7. Combine the noodles, stir-fried meat and vegetables with the chicken stock, toss well until evenly distributed.
8. Serve hot with some fish sauce on the side and fresh calamansi to squeeze over the top just prior to eating.

# VEGETABLE DISHES

Unlike other cuisines, the Filipino cuisine does not have a wide selection of vegetable dishes at first glance. Although if you look hard enough at the few vegetable laden dishes, you will find dried fish or a little pork has been used somewhere in the mix. *Laing* (simmered taro leaves) usually includes some fried pork, or baby shrimp, while lentil stew (*monggo*) will normally have salted dried fish (*tuyo*) mixed through. Although there are signs Filipinos are starting to prefer more vegetables in their diet, even today, it's still not easy to be a vegetarian in the Philippines.

Vegetable recipes are most often prepared as side dishes paired with their meat counterpart. Stir-fried squash, carrots, cabbage or chayote are often cooked simply with a hint of garlic and ginger and serve as side dishes to fried pork, fish and other meats. Kangkong or water spinach is popular, sautéed simply with garlic, or it may be prepared *adobo* style. Seaweed salads are a popular accompaniment to fresh seafood.

In the Philippines, vegetables does not just pertain to green leafy ones, but also include root crops, stems, tubers, fruits, seeds, plants, and even vines and palms are used in cooking. As a home chef, discovering how to use the banana heart (*puso ng saging*), and the range of starchy root crops like yam (*ube*), taro (*gabi*) and sweet potato (*camote*) in cooking and even desserts has been a really exciting journey. Meanwhile, fruits, in their unripe form, including green papaya, banana, mango, and jackfruit are also treated as vegetables in the cuisine.

As attitudes toward healthy diets and nutrition continue to change in the Philippines, there will be renewed focus by Filipino chefs on how to integrate Pinoy flavors into standalone vegetarian fare. In *Maputing Cooking*, I've experimented with Filipino style slaws, soups, salsas and salads. And at home, I tend to go without the meat or find vegetarian substitutes when it comes to *monggo*, chop suey or *pinakbet*. I truly believe pina *pinakbet* has all the flavor it needs without the *chicharon* or *bagnet*—just a little *bagoong* is fine ... oh wait, that's not vegetarian either!

# Filipino Chopsuey

It was once believed that the dish *chopsuey* originated in America, made by early Chinese immigrants in the U.S. It came from the word *tsap seui* (miscellaneous leftovers) and means it's a great, improvisation dish that every home chef should have in their repertoire. I was drawn to the recipe as it closely resembles Indonesian *cap cay* at first glance. But taking a closer look, there's a lot more going on in the Filipino version. For starters, a more global selection of vegetables can be added including carrots, snow peas, green beans, bell pepper, cauliflower, broccoli, cabbage and chayote. Shrimp or processed fish or squid balls can be added, along with chicken, pork, liver, gizzard or quail eggs. I never cook *chopsuey* the same way twice—it's inherently a dish suited to cleaning up whatever leftover vegetables or meat you have in the fridge.

**Good for 6–8**
**Prep time: 20 minutes**
**Cooking time: 25 minutes**

¼ cup (30 g) carrot, sliced into rings
¼ cup (30 g) chayote (*sayote*), sliced diagonally
1 cup (180 g) broccoli, cut into florets
1 cup (180 g) cauliflower, cut into florets
1 cup (150 g) snow peas, trimmed
3 tablespoons cooking oil
2 tablespoons chopped garlic
½ cup (80 g) chopped onion
¼ cup (30 g) sliced fresh or dried shiitake mushroom
5 oz (100 g) chicken liver, marinated in 2 tablespoons soy sauce
5 oz (100 g) shrimp, peeled and deveined
½ cup (125 ml ) water
3 tablespoons oyster sauce
1 cup (150 g) chopped cabbage
¼ cup (30 g) red bell pepper, sliced into strips
1 cup (120 g) baby corn, sliced in half
12 hard boiled quail eggs, peeled
2 tablespoons cornstarch, diluted in ¼ cup (60 ml) water
Salt and pepper, to taste

1. Prepare the vegetables, setting aside the cabbage, bell peppers, baby corn and mushroom, for blanching. Boil some water with salt in a pot on high heat and prepare some cold water in a large mixing bowl. Put the vegetables in the boiling water for 2–3 minutes, remove them and transfer them to the cold water to "shock" them. This will ensure that the color and crispness of the vegetables remain.
2. In a deep skillet, heat the oil and sauté the garlic and onion on medium heat for 2–3 minutes. Once fragrant, add the mushrooms followed by the chicken liver and shrimp. Toss to incorporate flavors for 2–3 minutes.
3. Pour in the water and oyster sauce and let it simmer until it bubbles. Add all the blanched vegetables followed by the cabbage, bell pepper, baby corn and quail eggs.
4. Mix everything and add the cornstarch slurry until the desired thickness is achieved. Adjust the seasoning by adding salt and pepper. Remove from the heat and do not allow the vegetables to overcook.

# Hearty Mung Bean Stew Ginisang Monggo

As a university student on a tight budget in Southeast Asia, I love to get a bargain and find the cheapest possible way to eat. Ginisang Monggo is the Philippines answer to lentil soup. Cheap, easy to make, delicious and extremely nutritious—there is nothing not to like about *monggo*—except perhaps the way it looks—a sort of mushy vegetable porridge. But while the basic *monggo* recipe can be a little bland, the secret is to add the bittersweet combo of squash and bitter gourd (*ampalaya*) or the leaves and top it off with some crispy dried fish (*tuyo*) or some *chicharon* bits which add salt and texture to the meal. I grow (*ampalaya*) in pots on my rooftop in Manila, so while I normally cook the fruit of the plant in *pinakbet* or with some eggs, I strip the leaves from the old *ampalaya* plant to go in my Ginisang Monggo, ensuring nothing from the garden goes to waste.

**Good for 6–8**
**Prep time: 10 minutes**
**Cooking time: 40 minutes**

1½ cups (300 g) dried mung beans
6 cups (1.5 l) water
2 tablespoons cooking oil
3 tablespoons chopped garlic
½ cup (80 g) chopped onion
2 medium tomatoes, chopped
1 cup (125 g) chopped squash
1 tablespoon fish sauce (*patis*)
Salt and pepper, to taste
2 bunches fresh bitter gourd (*ampalaya*) leaves (spinach leaves may be substituted)
5 oz (100 g) small dried fish (*tuyo/ danggit*)

1. Wash the mung beans under running water and remove any stones and impurities that float.
2. In a large pot, transfer the beans and add the water. Let it boil for 20–30 minutes or until the beans are tender and slightly mushy.
3. In a separate pan, heat the oil on medium heat and sauté the garlic, onion and tomatoes for 3–5 minutes or until fragrant. Add the squash and cook until tender.
4. Transfer the mixture to the large pot and let it simmer for 10 minutes, occasionally stirring to combine the mung beans mush with the mixture well. Season with fish sauce, salt and pepper.
5. Add in the bitter gourd leaves and small dried fish and simmer for another 5 minutes before serving.

# Roasted Eggplant Fritata
## Poque-Poque Pizza

I was sight-seeing in Laoag, Ilocos Norte when I first came across the *poque-poque* pizza. The local word for eggplant, this Ilocano dish uses roasted eggplant as the hero ingredient for a Filipino inspired vegetarian pizza. Interestingly, it is not a simple use of local ingredients to top a pizza, but rather uses a mixture of what is a sort of hybrid *ensaladang talong* or *tortang talong*—a train smash of eggplant, tomatoes, onions and eggs. This delightful soy-sauce infused mixture is then inexplicably (or perhaps ingeniously) ladled over a pizza base and topped with cheese and baked like a classic Italian pizza. Genre-defying, it's a sort of Asian infused breakfast pizza—however you define it, it's another delicious example of Filipino culinary experimentation over the years and easy to try out at home!

**Good for 6–8**
**Prep time: 20 minutes**
**Cooking time: 15 minutes**

6–8 eggplants, roasted and peeled
Cooking oil, as required
1 tablespoon chopped garlic
¼ cup (40 g) chopped onion
½ cup (100 g) chopped tomatoes
3 tablespoons tomato paste
½ cup (125 ml) water
Salt and pepper, to taste
5 eggs, beaten
2 tablespoons soy sauce
2 pieces 8-in (20-cm) round store-bought pizza base
2 cups (200 g) mozzarella or cheddar cheese, grated
Basil leaves, to garnish

1. Pre-heat oven to 350°F (180°C).
2. Roast the eggplants directly on a gas stove on high heat until the skin is charred on all sides. Use tongs in turning or hold the stem so you won't get burned. Peel the skin once cooled and set it aside.
3. In a shallow skillet, heat the oil and sauté the garlic, onion and tomatoes on medium heat for 3–5 minutes or until the tomatoes soften. Slightly mash the tomatoes and add the tomato paste and water until it is chunky. Season with salt and pepper and simmer for 2 minutes. Set the tomato mixture aside.
4. In another shallow skillet, add the roasted eggplant and the eggs. Stir gently until the consistency becomes similar to scrambled eggs.
5. Pour the soy sauce and season with salt and pepper. Set the eggplant mixture aside.
6. Get the pizza dough and start assembling the pizza. First, top it with the tomato mixture. Sprinkle with half of the grated cheese, and add the eggplant mixture on top. Finish it off by topping with the remaining cheese.
7. Bake in the oven for 10 minutes or until the cheese melts. Serve while hot, garnished with the basil leaves.

# "Adobo" Water Spinach
## Adobong Kangkong

In the Philippines there is very little that cannot be made *adobo* style—truly a method of cooking rather than a specific recipe, *Adobo* makes everything taste great. I love to make Adobong Kangkong when preparing a meal with several dishes. It's very easy to cook, uses readily available pantry items and a healthy addition to a meal laden with meat dishes. As a vegetarian dish, this definitely benefits from a little kick from the chilies, but one or two fiery bird's-eye chilies *siling labuyo* will be more than enough!

**Good for 3–4**
**Prep time: 5 minutes**
**Cooking time: 5 minutes**

1 tablespoon thinly sliced garlic
2 red bird's-eye chilies (*siling labuyo*), sliced thinly
2 tablespoons cane vinegar
2 tablespoons soy sauce
½ teaspoon cracked black peppercorns
4 tablespoons water
1 bunch (10 oz/300 g) water spinach (*kangkong*)
Cooking oil, as required

**1.** In a skillet or wok, heat a little cooking oil and fry the sliced garlic for two minutes or until fragrant and turning golden brown.
**2.** Add the thinly sliced chili, deseed it prior to slicing for a less spicy dish, sauté with the garlic for one minute
**3.** Add the vinegar, soy sauce, peppercorns and water, cooking and mix together well
**4.** Add the water spinach and toss it through the *adobo* mixture for 3–4 minutes, or until the spinach has wilted and reduced.
**5.** Serve with steaming white rice and grilled pork or seafood dishes.

# Filipino Vegetable Medley
## Pinakbet Ilocano

*Pinakbet,* sometimes shortened to *pakbet* is a popular dish that originated in the Ilocos region of Northern Luzon. This dish is a colorful medley of iconic tropical vegetables: squash, string beans, eggplant and bitter gourd *(ampalaya)* traditionally cooked in clay pots. Pre-chopped mixes of these vegetables are usually sold in the traditional market to save preparation time at home—and is how I first encountered the recipe. Although a predominantly vegetarian dish, *pakbet* has powerful flavors, the intense bitterness of the bitter gourd is offset by the sweetness of the squash, while saltiness is added from the *bagoong.* One of my vegetable *suki* (regular suppliers) was Ilocano and taught me to use the baby *ampalaya,* round shaped bitter gourds grown in the region, and Ilocano *bagoong isda* (a fish based fermented paste). The end result is a deliciously balanced vegetable medley, everything cooked to perfection. Filipinos generally garnish the dish with either *chicharon,* or *bagnet* (crisp fried pork belly), although at home I usually avoid adding these to keep the dish vegetarian, particularly if serving it with other meat dishes.

**Good for 6–8**
**Prep time: 10 minutes**
**Cooking time: 25 minutes**

2 tablespoons cooking oil
3 tablespoons chopped garlic
½ cup (80 g) chopped onion
½ cup (100 g) chopped tomatoes
¼ cup (60 g) fermented fish paste (*bagoong isda*), fermented shrimp paste (*bagoong alamang*) may also be used
1 cup (250 ml) water
2 cups (250 g) squash (*kalabasa*)
2 cups (250 g) round eggplants, cut into rounds
1 cup (120 g) baby bitter gourd (*ampalaya*), sliced into quarters (larger *ampalaya* can be used, sliced into half circles)
2 cups (250 g) okra, heads removed
2 cups (250 g) string beans, cut into 2 in (5 cm) lengths
2 cups (250 g) winged beans (*sigarilyas*), trimmed and cut in half
Salt and pepper, to taste
10 oz (300 g) crisp fried pork belly (*bagnet* or *lechon kawali*), to garnish

1. In a large pot, heat the oil and sauté the garlic and onion on medium heat. Add the tomatoes and fermented fish paste. Sauté for 5 minutes or until fragrant. Pour in the water and let it simmer for 3–5 minutes.
2. Next add the vegetables in the order of their cooking time. The idea here is to layer the ingredients, so the ones with longer cooking time sauté at the bottom of the pan, while at the top, the fresh greens are lightly cooked through steam and indirect heat. Start with the squash at the bottom—and give it a 5 minute head start before layering the eggplants, bitter gourd, okra, string beans and winged beans on top.
3. Let it cook for 10 minutes. Do not disrupt the layers by stirring, just shake the pot side to side once or twice while cooking.
4. Season the *pinakbet* with salt and pepper.
5. Serve the *pinakbet* with *bagnet, lechon kawali,* or some dried fish on top.

# Spicy Taro Leaves in Coconut Milk
## Laing

When people ask me to name my top five favorite Filipino dishes, *laing* always makes the list. Although this is a classic *ginataan* or coconut milk based recipe, if one has never experienced the earthy bitterness of taro leaves, it creates a lasting memory on the palate. Raw taro is mildly toxic, so it's essential that the leaves are first sun-dried prior to consumption. Once the leaves and stems have shriveled from drying, they can be torn into strips and used in cooking. As a Bicolano dish, *laing* is typically cooked with plenty of bird's-eye chilies (*siling labuyo*). To balance out the heat, the *laing* must be thick and creamy. So be sure to use only the first press if using fresh coconut, or coconut cream (as opposed to milk) if using the canned version. In Bicol, baby shrimp are usually added to *laing* and eaten whole, though in my version I prefer the texture of using larger shrimp chopped them into small cubes, this addss springy seafood overtures to the dish.

**Good for 6–8**
**Prep time: 10 minutes**
**Cooking time: 1 hour**

2 tablespoons cooking oil
2 tablespoons minced garlic
½ cup (80 g) chopped red onion
2 tablespoons grated ginger
3 tablespoons fermented shrimp paste (*bagoong alamang*)
1½ cups (375 ml) coconut cream
5 oz (150 g) dried taro leaves (*dahon ng gabi*)
½ cup (125 ml) water
2–3 red bird's-eye chilies (*siling labuyo*), or more according to your preference,
Salt and pepper, to taste

1. Heat the oil on medium heat in a deep skillet and sauté the garlic, onion and grated ginger. Once the onion is translucent and the ginger is fragrant, add the shrimp paste and the coconut cream. Simmer for 5 minutes.
2. Add the taro leaves and water. Cover with a lid and simmer for 30 minutes on medium heat until the leaves are tender.
3. Once the leaves are soft, add the chilies and adjust the taste by adding salt and pepper. Simmer for another 5 minutes.
4. Plate it up and serve with steaming white rice.

# Buffalo Cheese and Tomatoes on Toast

*Kesong puti* is a soft, unaged, white cheese made from unskimmed goat (*carabao*) milk, salt and rennet. This cheese originated from and is produced in the provinces of Bulacan, Cebu, Laguna and Samar. In the Philippines, it is a popular breakfast food eaten with the freshly baked local bread called *pan de sal*. In Sydney, fresh breakfasts of soft cheese, avocado and sourdough are a popular harborside breakfast—so this recipe puts a Filipino twist on a classic Aussie breakfast combo. Rich in milk fats and salt, cheese is a perfect partner for fresh tomatoes. Though where possible use sweeter cherry tomatoes for this dish, as the native Philippine tomato can be a bit too sour to enjoy raw with this dish. If you do use them, chop finely and consider adding some caramelized red onion to the recipe. Freshly picked basil, which grows easily in most parts of the world if you don't already have a pot on your windowsill, will take this to the next level!

**Good for 4–6**
**Prep time: 10 minutes**
**Cooking time: no cooking**

1 loaf sourdough bread (this recipe can also be used as a healthy filling for ordinary *pan de sal* as well)
10 oz (300 g) cherry tomatoes (try an assortment of yellow, red and choco tomatoes)
7 oz (200 g) *kesong puti*
Olive oil, to drizzle
Salt and pepper, to taste
½ cup (15 g) freshly picked basil leaves

1. With a bread knife, cut the sourdough bread into slices and toast lightly.
2. Halve or quarter the cherry tomatoes (depending on their size) into ½ in (12 mm) segment.
3. Spread a (.20 in/½ cm) thick layer of *kesong puti* over the sliced bread. Top with the tomatoes then drizzle with olive oil. Season with salt and pepper to taste.
4. With your hands, press and tear the basil leaves into small pieces and sprinkle them over the bread.

# Roasted Eggplant Torta
## Tortang Talong

*Tortang talong* is one of the first Filipino dishes I tried and is a favorite to prepare at home—with simple ingredients and relatively easy method. A sort of eggplant fritter, what sets it apart is that the stem of the eggplant is left intact, while the roasted flesh is splayed to create a mushy framework to bind together the egg and other ingredients when fried together in a pan. While typically focused more on the vegetables, *torta* can be made to a heavier standalone dish through the addition of meat or potatoes. My favorite preparation however uses *tinapa* or smoked fish which perfectly complements the smoky flavors of the roasted eggplant. In the Philippines, this is usually paired with tomato sauce or banana ketchup but if you find readymade sauces too sweet, I recommend whipping up your own fresh tomato sauce to serve on the side. Be sure to use cherry tomatoes here, not the native Philippine tomato which are a little too sour for this purpose.

**Good for 6–8**
**Prep time: 20 minutes**
**Cooking time: 10 minutes**

8 Asian eggplants
Cooking oil, as needed
2 tablespoons chopped garlic
½ cup (80 g) chopped onion
½ cup (120 g) diced potatoes
¼ cup (60 g) diced carrots
Salt and pepper, to taste
¼ cup (30 g) green peas
¼ cup (30 g) diced red bell
　pepper
2 cups (300 g) smoked fish
　(*tinapang bangus*), flaked
6 eggs, beaten
¼ cup (60 ml) water
Homemade Ketchup (page 32),
　to serve

1. Roast the eggplants directly on a gas stove on high heat until the skin is charred on all sides. Use tongs in turning or hold the stem so you won't get burned. Peel the skin once cooled, not removing the stem and set it aside.
2. In a shallow skillet, heat the oil and sauté the garlic and onion on medium heat for 2–3 minutes or until the onions are translucent. Add the potatoes and carrots and simmer for 3–5 minutes. Season with salt and pepper. Mix in the green peas and bell pepper. Toss for 5 minutes or until everything is cooked. Fold in the flaked smoked fish and set aside.
3. In a medium-sized mixing bowl, beat the eggs with the water. Season with salt and pepper.
4. On a large plate, lay one eggplant and gently mash the flesh with a fork. Make sure the stem will not be broken. Dip the flattened eggplant in the beaten eggs and top it with 2 tablespoons of the smoked fish mixture.
5. In a shallow skillet, heat some oil on medium heat. Get the eggplant and slide it directly in the pan in one swift motion. Cook one side for 3 minutes or until you see that the first side is set or cooked. Flip it swiftly by holding the stem with one hand and the other with the turner supporting the toppings so they won't fall off. Remove from the pan once the mixtures is set and cooked. Repeat the process with the remaining eggplants.
6. Serve it with steaming white rice and a side of Homemade Ketchup.

1. Roast the eggplant directly on a gas stove.

2. Lay the eggplant on a plate and gently mesh the flesh with a fork.

3. Fry the garlic, onion, potatoes, carrot, green peas and bell pepper for 5 minutes.

4. Top with 1–2 tablespoons of the smoked fish mixture.

5. Cook one side for 3 minutes or until the smoked fish mixture is set.

# SEAFOOD DISHES

As a rich and biodiverse archipelago blessed with thousands of kilometers of coastline, rivers and lakes, it is no wonder fish and seafood are a staple of the Filipino diet. There are a lot of species that can be found here like milk fish (*bangus*), tilapia, shrimps, lobsters, clams, crabs and crablets down to the smallest species like *sinarapan*, anchovies (*dilis*) and freshwater sardines (*tawilis*). The Philippines is a major exporter of seafood and renowned for Yellow Fin Tuna caught off the coastline of Mindanao. Fish eyes, shrimp heads and crab fat are also not spared. Even seaweeds are used in *enchiladas* or served as dipping sauce (*sawsawan*) or side flavorings.

Seafood are quick and easy to cook and were traditionally prepared in various ways such as steaming, boiling, grilling, frying or poaching in citrus juice or vinegar. As different culinary influences arrived in the Philippines over the centuries, *ginataan* or coconut milk based recipe, *rellenong* and *escabeche* were added in the mix.

Likewise, preserving seafood has been a custom for a long time and created new flavor possibilities in Filipino cooking. Seafood preservation is done by adding vinegar (*paksiw*), smoking the fish and drying under the sun. Shrimps can be fermented and made into *bagoong alamang*.

I love seafood best when fresh and cooked as simple as possible. Though I love the complexity of a perfectly prepared *kinilaw*, probably my all time favorite seafood meal in the Philippines was buying a piece of freshly caught marlin on a stick, cooked over hot coals on the side of the road in Camiguin for ten pesos. A squeeze of calamansi juice and I was in foodie heaven. With a few exceptions, in my seafood preparations I like to focus on light, fresh and make seafood the focus of the dish.

# Hong Kong Style Steamed Fish
## Steamed Itim Na Lapu-Lapu

I had my first steamed black grouper (*lapu-lapu*) at the *dampa palutuan* at Seaside in Pasay City. *Palutuan* is a great concept—literally meaning a place where you get your food cooked, you select from freshly caught fish at the adjacent market and then the restaurant cooks the seafood for you just charging a cooking fee and providing the extras like rice, salads and drinks. While the *palutuan* can prepare seafood in all the classic styles, sometimes I ask to take over in the kitchen and cook my own so I can play around with the flavors and ensure everything is just right. Looking for a change from fried fish with sweet or sour flavors, the steamed black grouper was perfect. Bearing much similarity to the style of seafood cooking in Hong Kong, the flavors here are light, subtle and balanced.

**Good for 2–4**
**Prep time: 10 minutes**
**Cooking time: 20 minutes**

1 piece (2–2.2 lbs/800 g–1 kg) fresh black grouper (*lapi-lapu*) or seabass, cleaned and scales removed
¼ cup (40 g) thinly sliced onion leeks
¼ cup (40 g ) thinly sliced ginger
¼ cup (40 g ) thinly sliced shiitake mushrooms (optional)
¼ cup (40 g ) chopped coriander leaves (cilantro)
¼ cup (60 ml) oyster sauce
2 tablespoons soy sauce
2 teaspoons sugar
1 teaspoon ground black pepper
¼ cup (60 ml) water
¼ cup (60 ml) canola oil
3 tablespoons sesame oil

**1.** Prepare the fish by cutting a diagonal slit in the middle part on both sides to allow the flavors to enter and infuse the fish.
**2.** Prepare the steamer. Fill a large pot with water, turn the heat to high and bring it to a boil.
**3.** On a deep ceramic plate that will fit the steamer, lay some onion leeks, ginger and mushrooms. Place the fish on top. Scatter more onion leeks, ginger and mushrooms on top of the fish. Top with some chopped coriander leaves. Set aside.
**4.** In a separate bowl, combine the oyster sauce, soy sauce, sugar, pepper and water to make the sauce. Pour it over the fish.
**5.** Once steam starts to rise, place the fish in the steamer and cook for 10–15 minutes. Set aside.
**6.** In a small pan, mix the canola and sesame oil and heat it for a 3–5 minutes on high heat or until it's piping hot. Turn off the heat and pour the oil over the steamed fish and top it with more fresh leeks and coriander leaves.
**7.** Serve sizzling hot with steaming white rice.

# Mud Crabs with Coconut
## Ginataang Alimango

While elsewhere in Southeast Asia, crabs are normally prepared in more savory, salty preparations that are often tomato, or oil based; the Philippines bucks this trend a little bit, instead pairing soft sweet crab meat with a thick, creamy coconut based sauce where squash and string beans impart a sweet and herbaceous flavor. Delicious on its own, it will often be served with spiced vinegar as dipping sauce (*sawsawan*), which cuts through the coconut cream and imparts some zing to the recipe. *Alimango* is the Filipino term for the common mud crab which should be used for this dish. Make sure you crack the crab claws before adding to the coconut cream base, so the sauce enters and infuses with the meat while cooking.

**Good for 6–8**
**Prep time: 15 minutes**
**Cooking time: 30 minutes**

4.5 lbs (2 kg) or around 2–3 live or pre-cooked mud crabs (*alimango*)
Cooking oil, as required
3 tablespoons chopped garlic
¼ cup (40 g) chopped onion
2 tablespoons thinly sliced ginger
3 cups (450 g) squash (Japanese or butternut), cut into 1-in (2.5-cm) chunks
1 cup (250 ml) water
1½ cups (375 ml) coconut cream (*kakang gata*)
2 cups (300 g) string beans, cut into 2-in (5-cm) lengths
3 tablespoons fish sauce (*patis*)
Salt and pepper, to taste
Filipino Style Spiced Vinegar (page 28), to serve

1. Prepare the crabs. If using live crab, you can put them to sleep in the freezer first, or else steam in a pot until cooked and the crab body has turned red. Remove and crack the claws. Cut the body into quarters. Remove the hairy lungs and wash thoroughly under running water. Set aside.
2. In a deep pot, heat the oil and sauté the garlic, onion and ginger on medium heat for 3–5 minutes. Once fragrant, add the squash, water and coconut cream. Cover and let it simmer for 15–20 minutes or until the squash is tender and the coconut cream begins to separate.
3. Add the string beans and cooked crab and mix well. Simmer for another 5 minutes.
4. Add the fish sauce and season with a little salt and pepper.
5. Serve with spiced vinegar and steaming white rice.

# Squid Adobo Adobong Pusit

While the variations on *adobo* are almost endless it's worth understanding some of the major categories of *adobo*—and Adobong Pusit or Squid Adobo is one of them. Visually, Adobong Pusit is much darker than the classic *adobo* as it's colored by the black squid ink and is soupier than usual. Chilies are normally added for a spicy kick when cooking *adobo* with squid. In the Philippines, the recipe normally uses baby squid, usually separated into two parts, the head/tentacles part (ink sack removed) and the main outer body. As they are quite small the entire squid is consumed. However, if using medium to large squid which is more common outside of the Philippines, you can cut out the eyes/beak and slice the body into rings.

**Good for 6–8**
**Prep time: 10 minutes**
**Cooking time: 20 minutes**

2 lbs (1 kg) squid baby or medium
   sized squid
¼ cup (60 ml) cooking oil
5 cloves garlic, chopped
1 medium onion, chopped
3 tomatoes, chopped
¼ cup (60 ml) vinegar
¼ cup (60 ml) soy sauce
½ cup (125 ml) water
3 long green chilies (*siling*
   *mahaba*)
Salt and pepper, to taste

1. In a large mixing bowl, wash the squid under running water to clean them. Remove the head along with the innards and feel for a hard, clear and plastic-like filament, tug it and pull it out. Set the squid and the tentacles aside.
2. In a shallow skillet, heat the oil and sauté the garlic, onion and tomatoes on medium heat for 2–3 minutes or until fragrant. Add the squid body, head and tentacles and sauté for 1 minute.
3. Add the vinegar, soy sauce and water. Simmer for 5 minutes. Do not simmer for a long time to prevent the squid from getting tough.
4. Add the green chilies and simmer for 2–3 minutes to give it a spicy kick. Season with salt and pepper.
5. Serve with steaming white rice.

# Shrimp in Spicy Coconut Milk with Jackfruit Ginataang Hipon

When it comes to cooking shrimp, Filipinos are prone to intensify the flavors of the dish through the incorporation of tropical fruits. I love to use bilimbi (*kamias*), one of the souring agents popular with Filipino stew (*sinigang*), which imparts a sour acidity that cuts through the coconut and balances the sweetness of the shrimp meat. Jackfruit (*langka*) is also popularly used as a partner to the sweet succulent shrimp. Take care not to overcook the shrimp; you'll want to gobble this delicious down so you want the shells to come off easily when it's time to eat!

**Good for 6–8**
**Prep time: 10 minutes**
**Cooking time: 30 minutes**

Cooking oil, as required
2 tablespoons chopped garlic
¼ cup (40 g) chopped onion
2 tablespoons thinly sliced ginger
¼ cup (40 g) finely chopped dried fish (*tuyo/danggit*)
3 cups (450 g) raw jackfruit (*langka*)
1½ cups (375 ml) coconut cream
1 cup (250 ml) water
2 lbs (1 kg) fresh shrimp (*suahe*)
2 tablespoons fish sauce (*patis*)
¼ cup (40 g) sliced long green chilies (*siling mahaba*)
Salt and pepper, to taste

**1.** In a shallow skillet, heat the oil and sauté the garlic, onion and ginger on medium heat for 3–5 minutes.
**2.** Add the dried fish and toss until fragrant. Mix in the jackfruit, coconut cream and water. Let it simmer for 10–15 minutes until the jackfruit is tender.
**3.** Once tender, add the shrimp (if preferred, the shrimp may be shelled first prior to adding) and season with the fish sauce, salt and pepper. Cover again for 5 minutes and turn off the heat once the shrimps turn to a nice color orange. Do not overcook the shrimps.
**4.** Top with the green chilies and serve while hot.

# Grilled Tuna

## Inihaw Na Panga Ng Tuna

The Philippines undoubtedly has some of the best fishing grounds in the world and is one of the best locations to catch Yellow Fin Tuna. In the Southern fishing port of General Santos, the best tuna in the world is landed and processed for sale. While most of the catch goes straight to Japan, Filipinos on the ground often buy whole Yellow Fin Tuna and air cargo it to Manila for use in restaurants, or celebrations. The best and most flavorsome part of any fish is usually found in the cheek or jaw. So you can imagine my delight the first time I tried a delicious grilled tuna jaw the size of a steak! Grilling over charcoal adds that smokey flavor although, you can also broil it in the oven or use an electric griller. A simple soy-calamansi marinade is common in the Philippines, which may be substituted, or complemented by a spicy chili-vinegar dipping sauce upon serving.

**Good for 6–8**
**Prep time: 10 minutes/marinate at**
  **1–2 hours or overnight**
**Cooking time: 20 minutes**

4.5 lbs (2 kg) tuna *panga*
⅓ cup (50 g) chopped garlic
1 tablespoon grated ginger
½ cup (125 ml) soy sauce
⅓ cup (80 ml) calamansi juice
2 tablespoons sugar
1 tablespoon ground black pepper
Soy and Calamansi Dipping Sauce (page
  30), for dipping

1. In a large mixing bowl, mix everything and marinate the tuna for at least 1–2 hours. To get the best result, marinate it overnight. Place in the refrigerator to maintain its freshness.
2. Prepare the griller and grill the tuna on each side for 10–15 minutes on medium heat or until well-cooked.
3. Serve the grilled tuna *panga* with Soy and Calamansi Dipping Sauce.

# Sweet and Sour Pan-Fried Grouper
## Escabescheng Lapu-Lapu Salad

One of the classic seafood preparations found in the Philippines is this sweet and sour whole fish (*Escabecheng Lapu-Lapu*). *Lapu-lapu* or grouper is favored here for its meaty white flesh that holds together well upon frying though you can also substitute tilapia or any other white fish, or even fillets. Visually, nothing beats the look of a fried red grouper set against the color medley of the *escabeche*. For me this is one of the recipes where restaurants in Manila will sometimes take shortcuts using cheap pre-made sauces which can result in an overly sweet or fluorescent red color in the final dish. Where possible go with fresh ingredients, and while in some parts of the world you may have to use canned pineapple, a fresh pineapple takes this to the next level.

**Good for 6–8**
**Prep time: 20 minutes**
**Cooking time: 30 minutes**

1 whole grouper (*lapu-lapu*), 2.2–2.5 lbs (1–1.2 kg), cleaned and scaled
Salt and pepper, to season the grouper
½ cup (60 g) flour
2 tablespoons cooking oil
2 tablespoons chopped garlic
½ cup (75 g) sliced white onion
¼ cup (40 g) ginger, cut into long thin strips (matchsticks)
¼ cup (40 g) carrots, cut into long thin strips (matchsticks)
½ cup (125 ml) vinegar
3 tablespoons brown sugar
2 tablespoons ketchup
¼ cup (40 g) green bell pepper, cut into long thin strips (matchsticks)
½ whole pineapple, chopped (canned pineapple may be substituted)
Salt and pepper, to taste
3 tablespoons cornstarch, dissolved in ¼ cup (60 ml) water
Cooking oil, as required

1. Clean the fish under running water. Dry with paper towels and season with salt and pepper. Put some flour on a large plate and dredge the fish in a light coating of flour.
2. In a shallow skillet, heat some oil and deep fry the fish for 5–10 minutes per side on medium heat or until crisp.
3. In another shallow skillet, heat some oil and sauté the garlic, onion and ginger on medium heat for 3–5 minutes. Once fragrant, add the carrots and let it cook for 2 minutes.
4. Add the vinegar, brown sugar and ketchup. Let it simmer for 5 minutes.
5. Throw in the bell pepper and pineapple chunks. Season with salt and pepper. Simmer for 5 minutes, stirring occasionally.
6. Thicken the sauce by adding the cornstarch slurry and let it simmer for another 5 minutes, until a thick, rich consistency is achieved.
7. On a serving platter, place the fried fish and pour the *escabeche* generously on top. Serve while hot with steaming white rice.

# Crispy Fried Marinated Milk Fish
## Pritong Bangus

A common breakfast option in the Philippines is fried milk fish (*bangus*), a marinated milk fish that is tender on the inside and crispy on the outside. Normally enjoyed with fried egg and garlic fried rice (*sinangag*)—known as *bangsilog* (portmanteau of *bangus*, *sinangag* and *itlog*), it's a great way to start the day. While preparing it yourself is incredibly easy to do at home, the classic vinegar, garlic, pepper marinade is widely available in Philippine supermarkets pre-marinated and is a good time saver. It also freezes quite well, so I always keep some pre-marinated milk fish (*bangus*) in the freezer for an easy cooked breakfast option on weekends. If you're eating it later in the day, try pairing it with a bitter gourd (*ampalaya*) salad, or some homemade *atchara*—delicious!

**Good for 6–8**
**Prep time: 1 hour**
**Cooking time: 20 minutes**

2 cups (500 ml) vinegar
½ cup (80 g) chopped garlic
1 tablespoon salt
2 tablespoons ground black pepper
2 lbs (1 kg) medium sized milk fish (*bangus*), butterflied and deboned (if milk fish is not available, try mullet, or flounder or sole fillets)
Cooking oil, for frying
Filipino Style Spiced Vinegar (page 28), to serve

**1.** In a large glass mixing bowl, mix together the vinegar, garlic, salt and pepper. Marinate the fish for an hour or overnight before frying. Marinated milk fish (*daing na bangus*) can be stored for 3–5 days in the fridge.
**2.** In a shallow skillet, heat the oil and fry the fish on both sides on medium heat for 5–10 minutes or until golden brown and crisp.
**3.** Serve with steaming white rice and a fried egg and Filipino Style Spiced Vinegar for breakfast, or with freshly made Bitter Gourd Salad (page 56 ).

# Chris Urbano's Tuna, Mango and Bitter Melon Salsa

This is an original recipe I developed to help explain the exquisite flavors of the Philippines to non-Filipino friends and family and one I often prepare during live cooking demonstrations. I had two goals in mind with this recipe: First to showcase the best in local Philippine ingredients; and second to highlight the balanced complexity of a typical Filipino recipe, all in a simple dish that a non-Filipino audience can readily appreciate. For me, the best ingredients in the Philippines are undoubtedly the seafood and the fruits. So as the basis for this dish I used General Santos Yellow Fin Tuna and a combination of the classic sweet mango and the less sweet, but more textured, local Indian mango. To this sweet/savory combo I add calamansi for sourness and bitter gourd (not too much!) for bitterness and a touch of heat from mild long green chili. Salt, pepper and olive oil hold it all together. This can be served as an appetizer or a healthy main course for anyone looking to experience all the Filipino flavors without the calories!

**Good for 3–4**
**Prep time: 15 minutes**
**Cooking time: 10 minutes**

2 cups (300 g) thinly sliced bitter gourd (*ampalaya*)
½ cup (125 g) salt, to season the bitter gourd
1 lb (500 g) fresh tuna, sliced into 1-in (2.5-cm) chunks
1 tablespoon salt, to season the tuna
3 tablespoons olive oil
2 cups (300 g) thinly sliced tomatoes
1 cup (150 g) Indian mango, sliced into strips
1 cup (150 g) ripe sweet mango, cut into chunks
¼ cup (40 g) chopped onion leeks
¼ cup (40 g) thinly sliced long green chilies (*siling mahaba*)
2 tablespoons cane vinegar
⅓ cup (80 ml) olive oil, to drizzle
¼ cup (60 ml) calamansi juice, to drizzle
Salt and pepper, to taste

1. In a small mixing bowl, combine the thinly slice bitter gourd with ½ cup of salt and set aside for 20 minutes or until the bitter gourd has sweated. Rinse and set aside.
2. In another mixing bowl, pat dry and then season the tuna chunks with salt.
3. In a shallow skillet, heat 3 tablespoons of olive oil and sear the tuna chunks for 2–3 minutes or until the tuna is cooked on the outside, but still a bit raw on the inside. Set aside.
4. In a large mixing bowl, combine all the other ingredients. Start with the salted *ampalaya*, followed by tomatoes, Indian mango and ripe mango, onion leeks, chilies and cane vinegar. Add the cooked tuna.
5. Drizzle with the olive oil, calamansi juice and season with salt and pepper to taste. Toss it and put it in the refrigerator for 15 minutes.
6. Serve, best paired with an off-dry (slightly-sweet) Riesling or Chenin Blanc which will offset the bitter gourd, complement the mangoes and pop from the hint of chil.

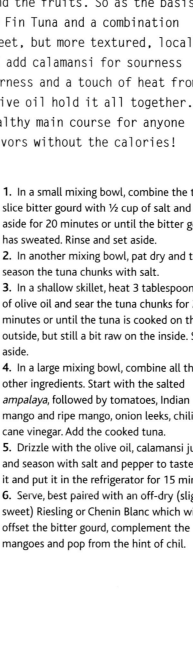

1. Sear the tuna chunks in a shallow skillet.

2. The tuna should be cooked on the outside but a little raw on the inside.

3. Combine all the other ingredients in a mixing bowl.

4. Add the cooked tuna.

5. Drizzle with olive oil, calamansi juice and seson with salt and pepper.

# POULTRY DISHES

A mainstay of the Filipino diet, chicken is eaten weekly by Filipinos across the country. Although there are a number or superb local preparations of chicken, a casual observer in the Philippines would quickly notice the country's love affair with fried chicken in particular. An American culinary influence, Filipinos have now indigenized this iconic US staple: double dredged, golden crispy and served with sweet tomato sauce or banana ketchup—and rice. Although widely available and popularized by national chains like Jollibee or Max's, fried chicken is a common dish prepared at home as well.

While sometimes there is nothing like the crunchy bite of perfectly fried chicken, I'm really drawn by the unique flavors of the Philippines culinary past. Tinolang Manok was once the number one chicken recipe in the Philippines. A humble, but hearty stew with vegetables, papaya or chayote, with bitter overtones from either chili or *malunggay* leaves, peppercorns and ginger, I like to cook mine with heaps of healthy greens, delicious in a classic chicken broth. Other flavorsome preparations like chicken *inasal* which uses lemongrass and annatto oil really show off the variety of Filipino cooking.

Other interesting preparations of chicken are the Spanish influenced *rellenong manok* and *pavo embuchado* (stuffing the chicken for feasting/fiesta). Ground chicken meat can be used in *lumpia shanghai*. The Philippines even has its own style of chicken curry that is probably most similar to the Japanese style of curry but with coconut milk. The methods for cooking chicken in the Philippines are every bit as diverse as the range of culinary influences that have passed through over the centuries.

# Ginger Chicken Soup with Green Papaya
## Tinolang Manok

*Tinolang manok* is known for its famous literary reference in *Noli me Tangere*, the famous novel by the Philippines national hero Jose Rizal. This is a nutritious and complete dish consisting of broth, meat and plenty of vegetables. Packed with nutrition, it is often compared to the classic chicken soup found in Western cuisines—and similarly considered a comfort food and the perfect convalescence food. It's also popular with lactating mothers, as it is usually supplemented with *malunggay* leaves which aids lactation. When served, guests are usually given calamansi and fish sauce to enhance the flavor according to their preference. *Tinolang manok* is a perfect dish for busy Pinoy families; easy to cook yet it's a complete meal that everyone will love.

**Good for 6–8**
**Prep time: 10 minutes**
**Cooking time: 45 minutes**

2 tablespoons cooking oil
2-in (5-cm) ginger, peeled and
   sliced into thin strips
2 tablespoons chopped garlic
½ cup (80 g) sliced onion
1 whole chicken, cleaned and cut
   into 12 pieces
1 lb (500 g) chicken livers, washed
   (optional)
1 tablespoon salt
1 tablespoon whole peppercorns
8 cups (2 l) water or chicken broth,
   if available
2 cups (450 g) green papaya or
   chayote, cut into wedges
1 cup (40 g) chili leaves/*malunggay*
   leaves, picked and washed
¼ cup (60 ml) fish sauce (*patis*), to
   serve
¼ cup (60 ml) calamansi juice, to
   serve

**1.** In a large pot, heat the cooking oil and sauté the ginger, garlic and onion.
**2.** Add the chicken and livers (if using it). Brown the chicken on all sides and season with salt and the peppercorns.
**3.** Pour in the water or chicken stock and bring to a boil. Lower the heat and simmer for 30 minutes, until the chicken is cooked.
**4.** Once the chicken is tender, add the green papaya and simmer for 5 minutes more.
**5.** Remove from the heat and add the chili leaves or *malunggay* leaves and allow to wilt in the heat of the soup.
**6.** Serve with steaming hot white rice and small sauce dishes of fish sauce and calamansi juice to be added at the table according to taste.

# Lemongrass and Tamarind Chicken Soup Sinampalukang Manok

*Sinampalukang Manok* is a soup dish that can taste a little similar to *sinigang* but instead uses chicken as the main component of the dish. Fresh, young tamarind leaves are used, in addition to the tamarind pods and lemongrass to impart the unique, sour, citrusy notes of this dish. As a considerably lighter soup than most Filipino stew (*sinigang*), this is a great alternative when one's appetite is suppressed or when looking for a healthier weeknight alternative—and it has a very fast cooking time. In this recipe, we will be using fresh tamarind but you can also use the powdered kind if the tamarind fruit is not available. While the recipe is portioned as a main meal, it's worth considering serving it as a side soup or starter with just a little (shredded) chicken for a dinner party.

**Good for 6–8**
**Prep time: 10 minutes**
**Cooking time: 45 minutes**

2 cups (400 g) of fresh tamarind pods (*sampalok*) or substitute equivalent of tamarind powder
2 cups (500 ml) water for boiling tamarind pods
¼ cup (60 ml) cooking oil
½ cup (80 g) chopped onion
3 tablespoons chopped garlic
3 tablespoons sliced ginger
1 whole chicken, cut into 8 pieces
¼ cup (60 ml) fish sauce (*patis*)
5 stalks lemongrass, thick white part only, crushed
8 cups (2 l) water or chicken stock
2 cups (250 g) green beans, cut into 2 in (5 cm) lengths
Salt and pepper, to taste

1. Prepare the Tamarind stock (if using fresh tamarind). In a small pot, add the fresh tamarind and add 2 cups of water. Let it simmer until cooked and soft. Mash the tamarind pulp and with a fine sieve, strain to remove the skin and seeds. Set the liquid aside.
2. In a big pot, heat the oil and sauté the onion, garlic and ginger until fragrant. Add the chicken pieces and let it brown on all sides. Season with fish sauce and pepper. Pound the lemongrass bulb and sauté with the chicken.
3. Add the water or chicken stock and let it simmer for 20–30 minutes. Skim off any scum around the pot.
4. Mix in the green beans and cook for 2–3 minutes. Pour in the Tamarind juice and season the dish with salt and pepper according to taste.
5. Serve it with hot steaming rice.

# Filipino Chicken Congee Arroz Caldo

The name Arroz Caldo is somewhat deceptive, hinting at Spanish origins for the Filipino classic rice porridge. However, this dish was being prepared in the Philippines well before the Spanish colonial period. Known as *lugaw* it is far more likely this dish is the product of the Chinese influence on Filipino food bearing strong resemblance to congee. Of course over the centuries of Spanish colonial rule, many local dishes were renamed by the colonizers and Arroz Caldo was born. This recipe is simple to make and perfect in cold weather. It's the ultimate comfort food when sick, the combination of chicken and plenty of ginger are restorative. I like to use a whole chicken chopped into aprroximately 12 pieces—cooking chicken on the bone imparts great flavor. But if cooking with chicken fillet, consider adding some natural chicken stock or an organic stock powder. While the rice porridge itself is intentionally bland, fresh calamansi juice, fish sauce, chopped onion leeks and crispy fried garlic flakes are added to elevate the flavor and add texture. I like to serve mine with a hard boiled egg for additional protein.

**Good for 6–8**
**Prep time: 10 minutes**
**Cooking time: 30 minutes**

Cooking oil, as required
½ cup (80 g) finely diced garlic
¼ cup (40 g) ginger, cut into thin strips
½ cup (80 g) finely chopped onion
1 whole chicken, cut into 12 pieces (or 1 lb/500 g diced chicken breast)
1 tablespoon fish sauce (*patis*)
1 teaspoon ground black pepper
8 cups (2 l) water
1 cup (160 g) uncooked rice
1 cup (160 g) uncooked glutinous rice
2 cups (500 ml) chicken stock (or equivalent in organic stock powder)
Optional toppings: hard boiled egg, fried garlic, chopped green onions (scallions), calamansi juice and fish sauce (*patis*)

1. In a large cooking pot, fry half of the garlic in oil until crispy and golden brown. Remove and set aside, retaining the garlic infused cooking oil in the pot.
2. In the same pot sauté the ginger, remaining garlic and onion until brown. Add the chicken pieces and sauté until browned. Season with the fish sauce and pepper.
3. Add the water and let it boil. Add both types uncooked rice and stir continuously until the rice is cooked. You can simmer off water, or add more water or chicken stock as required to reach a porridge like consistency.
4. Serve the Arroz Caldo in bowls. Top it off with your choice of toppings: hard boiled egg, fried garlic, green onions and fresh calamansi juice.

# Bicol Style Chicken in Spicy Coconut
## Ginataang Manok Bicolano

A lot of my cooking is influenced by my favorite culinary region of the Philippines, Bicol. Having traveled widely in Southeast Asia, especially Indonesia, I love red hot spicy dishes and coconut based curries. So I was delighted when one of my *kasambahay* (house helpers) who was from Bicol served the perfect, spicy *ginataan manok* a few years back. Key to preparing a Bicol style chicken curry is the use of turmeric which gives the distinctive yellow color and the liberal use of red and green chilies both in simmering and fresh on top as a garnish according to one's taste. I love the cost effectiveness of this dish as well, green papaya or chayote are cheap. If you don't have fresh coconuts on hand the canned coconut cream is readily available in most grocery stores. Don't underestimate that little hint of bitterness from the greens—a little spinach can be substituted if you don't have *malunggay* or chili leaves on hand. This dish is hearty, warming and creamy with some spicy kick-try it!

**Good for 6–8**
**Prep time: 10 minutes**
**Cooking time: 45 minutes**

2 tablespoons cooking oil
2 in (5 cm) ginger, peeled and sliced into thin strips
2 tablespoons chopped garlic
½ cup (80 g) sliced onion
1 whole chicken (3 lbs/1½ kg), cleaned and cut into 12 pieces
1 tablespoon salt
1 tablespoon whole peppercorns
1 cup (250 ml) water or chicken broth
1½ cups (375 ml) coconut cream (*kakang gata*)
2 teaspoons ground turmeric
2 cups (450 g) green papaya or chayote, peeled and cut into wedges
4–6 long green chilies (*siling mahaba*), thinly sliced
1 cup (30 g) chili leaves/*malunggay* leaves (or spinach), picked and washed
¼ cup (60 ml) fish sauce (*patis*)
2–3 red bird's-eye chilies (siling labuyo), finely chopped (optional)

1. In a large pot, heat the cooking oil and sauté the ginger, garlic and onion.
2. Bring the pot to high heat before adding the chicken and browning it on all sides. Season with salt and whole peppercorns while it cooks.
3. Pour in the water or chicken broth, coconut cream and ground turmeric and bring to a boil. Then lower the heat and simmer for 25–30 minutes, or until the coconut cream begins to separate.
4. Add the green papaya (or chayote) and the sliced long green chilies and simmer for 5 minutes more until cooked.
5. Add the chili leaves or *malunggay* leaves and sit through until wilted from the heat of the stew. Season with fish sauce—you can vary the amount to taste.
6. Sprinkle with finely chopped bird's-eye chilies, if using, and serve with plenty of white rice and water— you're going to need both!

# Pinikpikan Chicken Stew

Pinikpikan is a dish originating in the Cordillera region of Northern Luzon. This dish is controversial in the Philippines as the traditional preparation involves beating a live chicken to death with a stick prior to charring the outside in a fire, and then combining it with mountain grown vegetables and locally-brewed rice wine to make a hearty stew. Normally prepared in ceremonial contexts such as ancestor worship, or when seeking spiritual blessings or favors, the traditions of the dish reflect the animistic beliefs and traditions of the Philippines which have survived into the modern age; however it is now very rare to see this dish prepared outside of a handful of locations in the Cordillera. In my version, I do not practice the beating or burning stages, but instead focus on the unique flavors of the dish. The dish is quite remarkable as it incorporates salted, smoked pork or *etag* and rice wine along with the chicken, so it represents a sort of Southeast Asian *coq a vin* conceived prior to European colonization.

**Good for 6–8**
**Prep time: 15 minutes**
**Cooking time: 45 minutes**

1 whole chicken cleaned and cut into
   12 pieces
3 cloves garlic, diced
1-in (2.5-cm) piece ginger, sliced thinly
1 onion, diced
2 stalks celery, sliced
Cooking oil, as required
8 cups (2 l) water
10 oz (300 g) *etag* (or bacon), sliced into
   thin pieces
1 cup (250 ml) rice wine
2 chayote, sliced
1 bunch of *pechay*, sliced

1. Using a cleaver or large chef's knife, dismember the chicken into around 12 pieces. For a more authentic, smokey taste you can chargrill the outside of the chicken over a charcoal, or using a kitchen blow torch, prior to cutting it up.
2. In a saucepan, sauté the garlic, ginger, onion and celery in a little cooking oil. Add the water and chicken pieces and bring to a boil. Simmer for 10 minutes or until the chicken meat is cooked.
3. Add the *etag* or bacon and rice wine and simmer for a further 10 minutes or until the bacon is tender and cooked.
4. Add the chayote and continue simmering for a further 7–8 minutes or until cooked through.
5. Add the *pechay* and simmer for a further 1–2 minutes or until it has wilted.
6. Serve with steaming white rice.

# Filipino Crispy Fried Chicken
## Kaligayahaan Ng Manok

Crispy fried chicken was introduced to the Philippines by the Americans and Filipinos quickly tweaked the dish slightly for the local palate. Double dredged and served with sweet tomato sauce and rice—it took off, and is now one of the most commonly eaten foods in Filipino homes, and fast food establishments alike. It was so successful that the number one fast food chicken comes from a homegrown fast food chain, Jollibee's Chickenjoy, trumping US chains McDonalds or KFC. In 2014, I released a funny video of me ordering Chickenjoy in Manila, but calling it instead by a deep Tagalog expression "Kaligayahan ng Manok" (Literally, the Joy of Chicken). Filipinos found the joke hilarious and the video was viewed millions of times by Pinoys. After the success of that video, I knew I had to make my take on this fast food classic, which I humbly call Kaligayahan ng Manok to this day.

**Good for 6–8**
**Prep time: 20 minutes**
**Cooking time: 30 minutes**

5 lbs (2.5 kgs) of chicken, chopped into large pieces (preferably thighs and drumsticks)
1 tablespoon salt, to season
1 cup (130 g) all-purpose flour
1 cup (110 g) cornstarch
1 tablespoon five spice powder
1 tablespoon garlic powder
1 teaspoon pepper
3 eggs
½ cup (125 ml) milk
Cooking oil, as required for shallow frying (around 1 cup/250 ml)
Homemade Ketchup (page 32), to serve

1. Pat dry the chicken and season with salt.
2. In a mixing bowl, combine the flour, cornstarch, five spice powder, garlic powder and pepper.
3. Dredge the chicken in the flour mixture and make sure the chicken piece is well coated. Shake off the excess flour.
4. In another mixing bowl, combine the eggs and milk and whisk into an egg wash.
5. Coat each piece of chicken thoroughly in the egg wash. Then dredge for a second time in the flour mixture ("double dredging").
6. In a deep skillet, pour oil to a depth of ½ to 1 inch (2.5 cm), sufficient to shallow fry the chicken. Heat the oil to 350°F (180°C). Gently place 3–4 pieces of chicken at a time and shallow fry it for 15–20 minutes on medium heat, until crispy and golden, turning once during cooking. Be patient, we do not want raw meat inside.
7. Once done, place it over a rack or on paper towels to drain excess oil. Serve with a simple Homemade Ketchup.

# Filipino Style Chicken Curry

One of the lesser known cultural influences in the Philippines comes from India, and Filipinos have evolved their own take on Indian curry. While most people associate Indian curry with being very spicy, the Filipino adaptation is decidedly non-spicy. It's also a more global fusion dish, combining a number of root crops and vegetables that reached the Philippines from Central America, with the curry powder that arrived from India. As a result, it much more resembles the simple Japanese curries often served along pork or chicken *katsu*. Although in my view, there is a lot more going on in the Filipino curry, reflecting the diverse range of spices and vegetables Filipinos cook with on a daily basis.

**Good for 6–8**
**Prep time: 10 minutes**
**Cooking time: 45 minutes**

2 tablespoons cooking oil
2 tablespoons minced garlic
½ cup (80 g) chopped red onion
2 tablespoons grated ginger
1 stalk celery, chopped
1 whole chicken, cleaned and cut into 12 pieces
1 cup (120 g) potato, cut into chunks
1 cup (120 g) carrot, cut into chunks
3 bay leaves
3 tablespoons yellow curry powder or curry paste
1½ cups (375 ml) coconut cream
2 tablespoons fish sauce (*patis*)
1 cup (250 ml) water
1 green bell pepper, deseeded and sliced
Red bird's-eye chilies (*siling labuyo*) (sliced), to taste
Salt and pepper, to taste

1. In a deep skillet, heat the oil and sauté the garlic, onion, ginger and celery. Add the chicken and cook on all sides until brown.
2. Throw in the potatoes, carrots, bay leaves and curry powder. Mix until fully coated with the curry powder. Add the coconut cream, fish sauce and water and let it simmer until the chicken is tender and the vegetables are cooked and the coconut cream has reduced.
3. Add the bell pepper and season to taste. You can add red chilies according to your taste.
4. Serve with steaming white rice.

# Chargrilled Lemongrass Chicken Chicken Inasal

Chicken Inasal came from Bacolod, a Visayan Region in the Philippines. Coming from the Spanish word *asar* meaning "to roast", the Bacolodnons adapted the word *inasal* meaning "to grill". Authentic Chicken Inasal uses native vinegar, lemongrass and spices and gets its famous color from using Annatto (*atsuete*) Oil for basting as it is grilled over hot coals (*uling*). While the marinade itself is not spicy, inasal is usually served with Soy and Calamansi Dipping Sauce (Toyomansi), see page 30, so it's left to the diner how spicy they like the dish. Usually cooked on a thick bamboo skewer to enable grilling over the hot coals, for home chefs, I find an electric griller, or even a panini press a great way to cook it, ideally something that can be easily opened to regularly baste the chicken to retain moisture and ensure the unique inasal yellow color is imparted. Smaller, native chickens are favored for their greater flavor, though any store bought chicken will still be delicious when prepared right.

**Good for 4**
**Prep time: 10 minutes/Marinade for 24 hours**
**Cooking time: 20–30 minutes**

½ cup (80 g) chopped garlic
2 teaspoons ground black pepper
¼ cup (60 ml) calamansi juice
1 cup (70 g) chopped lemongrass
½ cup (125 ml) cane or coconut vinegar
2 tablespoons salt
1 whole chicken, quartered
4 large bamboo skewers (if cooking on an open grill)
Pickled Papaya (page 29), to serve
Soy and Calamansi Dipping Sauce (page 30), to serve

**ANNATTO OIL**
1 tablespoon annatto seeds
½ cup (125 ml) cooking oil

1. Combine half of the garlic, black pepper, calamansi juice, lemongrass, vinegar and salt. Add the chicken pieces and marinate overnight or at least an hour.
2. Prepare the Annatto Oil by frying the annatto seeds in the oil for 5–10 minutes. Strain and set aside.
3. Make the basting sauce by frying the remaining garlic in the Annatto Oil until lightly toasted.
4. Skewer each quarter piece chicken in the bamboo skewers and grill on an open fire using charcoal or bake in the oven. When using the oven, use the broiler and put the chicken 6 inches (15 cm) below the oven heal element.
5. Baste the chicken pieces with the garlic infused Annatto Oil and turn every now and then until fully cooked and the juices run clear.
6. Serve with garlic fried rice (*sinangag*), Pickled Papaya (Atchara) and Soy and Calamansi Dipping Sauce (Toyomansi). Enjoy!

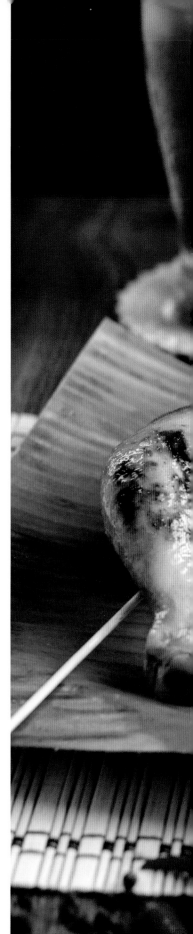

1. Prepare the marinade a day before.

2. Add the chicken pieces and marinade overnight or at least an hour.

3. Make the basting sauce by frying the garlic in the Annatto Oil.

4. Baste the chicken pieces with the garlic infused Annatto Oil.

5. Grill the chicken pieces until fully cooked and the juices run clear.

# PORK DISHES

When it comes to the heavier, main courses of a Filipino meal, meats such as pork, beef are where the chef turns their mind to. In some regions, *carabao* or goat can be substituted for beef. Mixing pork and chicken, often with liver, is also a common practice.

A Filipino's love for pork goes far, wide and back. A big chunk of Filipino cuisine uses pork as the main ingredient. There's pork chop, fried pork belly (*lechon kawali*), deep-fried pig trotters (*pata*), *menudo* (a traditional stew from the Philippines) and of course *adobo*. Almost no part gets thrown out. Innards are grilled and are eaten as street foods, the skin is deep-fried and are made into crunchy *chicharon*, the pig's head is prepared into sizzling *sisig* and even the pig's blood is made into *dinuguan* (a sort of black pudding and a local favorite).

The locals' love for pig traces back to Spanish's love for pork. When the Spaniards came to the country, they brought with them cattle and pigs. Pigs thrived more in their new habitat compared to cattle. They breed easily, are cheaply maintained and their food source can be as simple as leftovers from different households. As such the Spanish influence is particularly evident when it comes to pork, not more than with the prevalence of the Philippines answer to chorizo—*longganisa*. Found across Luzon, every township has their own unique preparation. *Tocino* meanwhile is a cured pork bacon using local ingredients to preserve the meat and impart flavor.

# Classic Chicken and Pork Adobo

## Adobong Baboy At Manok

*Adobo* is really a method of cooking rather than a specific recipe—and every region and even every family will have their own unique way of making *adobo*. In Manila, I've been asked to judge a number of *adobo* cooking competitions where enthusiastic home chefs showcase strange and wonderful takes on the dish—I've seen people include wild card ingredients from chocolate, to turmeric to watermelon to rum. And while this immense variety of *adobo* is great, it also presents a challenge to the wider adoption of Filipino cuisine or explaining people what this dish really is. So the "version" of *adobo* I present here is my attempt at distilling what is the classic "standard" recipe, which contains the essential ingredients and methodology of the dish. Pork belly is the classic meat to use, but for a less fatty dish, go for pork shoulder and I like to throw in a few hard boiled eggs. I recommend starting out by cooking it this way, and then adding your own little touch over time. When I cook this "down under" in Australia, I'll always sneak in a little vegemite, and it works pretty well with salt water crocodile meat as well!

**Good for 6–8**
**Prep time: 10 minutes**
**Cooking time: 45 minutes**

2 tablespoons cooking oil
¼ cup (40 g) pounded and chopped garlic
1 lb (500 g) chicken, cleaned and cut into 6–8 pieces
1 lb (500 g) pork (pork belly, or shoulder, cut into 2 in/5 cm cubes or *adobo* cut)
½ cup (125 ml) vinegar
½ cup (125 ml) soy sauce
1 tablespoon black whole peppercorns
3–5 bay leaves
1 cup (250 ml) water
6 hard boiled eggs

1. In a shallow skillet, heat the oil and sauté the garlic. Sear the chicken on medium heat for 5–10 minutes or until brown and remove from the pan. Add the pork and sear the meat on medium heat for 5–10 minutes or until brown on all sides. Remove the pork from the skillet. Set aside.
2. Add the vinegar, soy sauce, whole peppercorns, bay leaves and water to the skillet. Put back the chicken and pork and let it simmer for 30 minutes on low heat.
3. Once the meat is tender, add the hard boiled eggs and simmer for another 5 minutes. Remove from the stove.
4. Serve while still hot with steaming white rice.

# White Adobo
## Adobong Puti

This is a simpler version of the classic *adobo* most often associated with the Visayas region on the Philippines. It is called *puti* (meaning "white") because it doesn't use soy sauce that normally gives the dish its brown color—and this is likely the first way Filipinos cooked *adobo*, prior to the arrival of soy sauce from China. With the dominant flavor of vinegar in this dish, this really works best using exclusively a fatty pork cut—pork belly (*liempo*) is perfect instead of a leaner mixture of chicken and pork used in my classic *adobo* recipe. Adobong Puti is normally simmered until its almost dry and only a thick oily reduction remains. Probably the best Adobong Puti I ever had was to refry any leftovers in hot oil, locking in all the flavors and adding a crispy texture. Served with some thinly sliced green chilies—a great way to give new life to any leftovers!

**Good for 6–8**
**Prep time: 10 minutes**
**Cooking time: 45 minutes**

2 tablespoons cooking oil
¼ cup (40 g) pounded and
  chopped garlic
2 lbs (1 kg) pork belly, cut into
  2-in (5-cm) cubes (*adobo* cut)
⅓ cup (80 ml) vinegar
¼ cup (60 ml) fish sauce (*patis*)
1 cup (250 ml) water
3 bay leaves
1 tablespoon black whole
  peppercorns

**1.** In a shallow skillet, heat the oil and sauté the garlic. Sear the pork on medium heat for 5–10 minutes or until brown on all sides
**2.** Deglaze the pan with vinegar and fish sauce. Pour in the water and add the bay leaves and peppercorns. Let it simmer for 20–30 minutes until the meat is tender and the sauce has been significantly reduced.
**3.** Serve with steaming white rice.

# Streetside Pork Barbecue Skewers

Marinated pork, skewered and barbecued to perfection over open coals, with a zing of spicy vinegar—all for just a few pesos per stick! While the Philippines is not the first place to come up with the idea of cooking meat on skewers, two things set it apart from those found elsewhere in Asia. First is the addition of a succulent piece of pork fat as the first piece on the skewer. While the skewer of meat is cooking, this releases fats which spreads to the rest of the meat to keep it moist. It's also a delicious, sinful last bite! The second thing is the marinating and basting process, which is kind of an improvised affair using items found in the modern urban environment. A can of soft drink for sweetness, factory made banana ketchup imparts tang and a fluorescent color to the meat. While nothing beats an open charcoal fire for flavor, you can get great results on an electric grill, a panini press, or through broiling in the oven.

**Good for 6–8**
**Prep time: 1 hour**
**Cooking time: 20 minutes**

10–15 cloves garlic, minced
¼ cup (60 ml) soy sauce
¼ cup (50 g) brown sugar
1 cup (250 ml) lemon lime soda
¼ cup (60 ml) banana ketchup
¼ cup (60 ml) vinegar
1 tablespoon pepper
1 tablespoon salt
2 lbs (1 kg) pork shoulder (*kasim*) with fat still on (sliced ½-in/1-cm thick, fat removed, sliced into cubes)
15–20 bamboo skewers, soaked in water
Pickled Papaya (page 29), to serve

1. In a large mixing bowl, combine the garlic, soy sauce, brown sugar, soda, banana ketchup and vinegar for the marinade. Season with salt and pepper.
2. Add the meat and fat. Make sure to evenly coat it with the marinade. Refrigerate overnight.
3. Soak the bamboo sticks in water 30 minutes before grilling to prevent them from burning.
4. Skewer a piece of fat followed by 4–5 pieces of meat or until the skewer is full. Thread it carefully to the stick and make sure that the meat are compressed and tightly fastened
5. On an open charcoal grill, or electric grill, place the skewers and barbecue for 5–10 minutes on each side or until cooked through. While it cooks, baste it with the marinade from time to time.
6. Serve with rice and a side of Pickled Papaya (Atchara).

# Minced Pork with String Beans
## Giniling Na Baboy At Sitaw

This is one of my go to mid-week convenience dishes—you can whip it up in less than half an hour and it uses all ingredients commonly found in anyone's fridge. *Sitaw* or string beans grow really well even in the urban environment of Manila and I've always got a few plants in my rooftop garden. While this will still taste pretty good whatever beans you use, trying it with farm fresh picked beans and you'll see this dish in a whole new light. The simplest dishes are really more about the sourcing of great ingredients, than the actual cooking. So if you haven't tried growing your own beans at home—now is the time to try it out!

**Good for 6–8**
**Prep time: 10 minutes**
**Cooking time: 20 minutes**

3 tablespoons cooking oil
3 tablespoons chopped garlic
½ cup (80 g) chopped onion
½ cup (80 g) chopped tomatoes
½ lb (250 g) ground pork
¼ cup (60 ml) soy sauce
½ cup (125 ml) chicken stock or water
4 cups (500 g) string beans, cut into
    2-in (5-cm) lengths (green beans or
    *Baguio* beans can be used)
Salt and pepper, to taste

1. In a shallow skillet, heat the oil and sauté the garlic and onion on medium heat until fragrant. Add the tomatoes and cook for 3–5 minutes or until the tomatoes become tender.
2. Add the ground pork and cook for 10 minutes until browned. Pour the soy sauce and stock and simmer the dish for a further 5 minutes.
3. Throw in the beans and toss to mix thoroughly, simmer for a further 5 minutes.
4. Adjust the taste by seasoning with salt and pepper.
5. Serve with steaming white rice.

# Sydneysider Longganisa Baked Eggs
## Longsilog With A Twist

*Longsilog* with a twist—this is a great way to reimagine the all-time classic Filipino breakfast of Longganisa, Sinangag and Itlog (Longganisa with Rice and Eggs). I lived in Sydney, a cosmopolitan hotbed with dozens of different communities all adding something to the city's cuisines, for a few years. One thing I miss from the Sydney breakfast menu is baked eggs, which was a take on eggs found in Mediterranean and Northern African cooking. So this dish is a homage to the multicultural cooking scene in Sydney but adapted for the Philippines. I find the small, savory Vigan *longganisa* works best. Remember to cook everything in one pan as the fat and juices from the *longganisa* flavor the whole dish. This dish looks visually stunning and is deceptively easy to make! I serve mine with thick cut sourdough acknowledging the Sydney influence, but if you can't bear to have your *longganisa* without rice, a side of (garlic fried rice) *sinangag* will be equally delicious!

**Good for 4**
**Prep time: 10 minutes**
**Cooking time: 30 minutes**

Cooking oil, as required
10–12 pieces Vigan *longganisa* (or any other savory pork or beef sausage), cut into bite-sized pieces
½ teaspoon ground black pepper
1 teaspoon ground cumin
½ teaspoon smoked paprika
2 teaspoons finely chopped garlic
½ cup (40g) diced brown onion
15–20 cherry tomatoes, sliced in halves
1 can (10 oz/300 g) red kidney beans
3–4 eggs
Parsley, chopped (to garnish)
1 loaf sourdough bread, sliced

**1.** In a shallow skillet, fry the *longganisa* for 8–10 minutes or until cooked through and oils have been released. Add the pepper, cumin and paprika, and stir through.
**2.** Add the garlic and onion. Sauté for 3–5 minutes or until it turns translucent. Then add the cherry tomatoes and black pepper. Sauté for a further 3–5 minutes until softened.
**3.** Add the kidney beans. Once it's cooked, create little craters in the pan and crack the eggs into the craters.
**4.** Take the pan off the stove and place it in the oven. Check the dish every few minutes. Once the eggs are cooked, take it out of the oven. Garnish with chopped parsley for added flavor.
**5.** Serve with sourdough bread and a steaming cup of hot coffee for that perfect breakfast.

# Classic Pinoy Breaded Pork Chops

A simple classic, there are few things as satisfying as a well cooked pork chop for dinner. The classic Filipino pork chop is all about the marinating—so don't skip out on this step—and its really best to leave it overnight in the fridge for maximum flavor. It's hard to go wrong when it comes to the cooking. Pork chops are usually breaded in the Philippines (a great way to use up any old *pandesal*!) but for the health conscious, skip the double dredging in favor of a thin coat of cornstarch—or no breading at all. I like to serve this with Filipino Style Calamansi Slaw and of course a side of Atchara will complement this nicely as well.

**Good for 4–6**
**Prep time: 15 mins + time to marinate**
**Cooking time: 25 minutes**

2 lbs (1 kg) pork chops
½ cup (125 ml) soy sauce
10–12 cloves garlic, diced
⅓ cup (80 ml) freshly squeezed calamansi juice
   lime juice can be substituted)
2-in (5-cm) ginger, peeled and sliced thinly
1 cup (130 g) flour
2 eggs
½ cup (125 ml) milk
1 cup (125 g) bread crumbs
Cooking oil, for frying
Filipino Style Calamansi Slaw (page 57), to serve
Pickled Papaya (page 29), to serve

1. In a large mixing bowl, marinate the pork chops with the soy sauce, garlic, calamansi juice and ginger for at least two hours. For best results, marinate it overnight.
2. Prepare the breading station. Get three medium-sized bowls and put the flour in the first bowl. Whisk the eggs and milk together, in the second bowl, to create an egg wash. Put the bread crumbs in the third bowl.
3. In a shallow skillet, heat the oil for frying the pork chop.
4. With a clean hand, get a piece of pork chop and go through the breading process. First, dredge it in the flour, then dip it in the liquid egg wash, and finally in the bread crumbs.
5. Fry the pork chops on medium to low heat for 4–6 minutes on each side or until it turns golden brown. Once done, transfer them on a plate lined with paper towels to drain the excess oil for a minute or two.
6. Serve with a healthy fresh Filipino Style Calamansi Slaw or Pickled Papaya.

# Braised Pork with Black Beans and Pineapple Humba

Humba is a Bisayán recipe cooked widely across the Visayas region and parts of Mindanao. Just like *adobo*, *humba* was made due to the need to preserve meat for longer—and at first glance contains a number of similar ingredients and procedure as *adobo*. But what's really interesting about this dish is the texture, and much more powerful contrasts of flavors—which is achieved through the addition of fresh chunks of sweet pineapple, the concentrated saltiness of fermented black soybeans (*taosi*) and the stringy flesh of banana heart. While blackbeans keep well in tins, you'll really notice the difference if you use fresh pineapple in the dish. If you don't live in the tropics, artichoke is a decent substitute for banana heart. I actually find *humba* more interesting dish than *adobo*. It's a little more work, but a great dish to highlight the diversity of Filipino food.

**Good for 6–8**
**Prep time: 10 minutes**
**Cooking time: 60 minutes**

Cooking oil, as required
5 cloves garlic, minced
1 medium onion, sliced into rings
2 lbs (1 kg) pork belly
½ cup (50 g) brown sugar
½ fresh pineapple, cut into chunks (canned pineapple can be used)
10 oz (300 g) banana heart, soaked in water (or artichoke)
½ cup (125 ml) soy sauce
½ cup (125 ml) red cane vinegar (or any white vinegar can be substituted)
1 cup (250 ml) water
15–20 whole black peppercorns
6 bay leaves
½ cup (80 g) fermented black soybeans (*taosi*), soaked in water for 30 mins and drained prior to using

1. In a cooking pot, heat up the oil and sauté the garlic and onion on medium heat.
2. Add the pork and brown sugar and braise the pork for 5–10 minutes.
3. Add the pineapple chunks and banana heart and simmer for 5 minutes until softened.
4. Add the soy sauce, vinegar, water, peppercorns, bay leaves and fermented black soybeans and stir through.
5. Cook on low heat for at least 30 minutes to tenderize the meat and consolidate the flavors. If you have the time, continue cooking up to two hours. This can be nice to serve with the meat falling apart from extended cooking.

# Spicy Pork Belly in Coconut
## Bicol Express

This is a timeless classic in Filipino cooking that hails from the Bicol region known for its use of fiery red bird's-eye chilies (*siling labuyo*) and coconut cream (*gata*) in cooking. The pork is first seared among aromatic flavors and *bagoong*, before being simmered in coconut cream along with plenty of chilies. Be sure to use the thickest coconut cream, or the "first press" if using fresh coconuts. You need a thick creamy reduction to help neutralize the heat of the chilies. Why Bicol express? I've heard that when served at the correct level of spiciness, it's akin to having a steam train travel down one's throat—or that it will send one on an express trip to the bathroom the next day. You have been warned! Feel free to pare back the chilies if serving to people less accustomed to spicy foods.

**Good for 6–8**
**Prep time: 10 minutes**
**Cooking time: 45 minutes**

2 lbs (1 kg) pork belly (*liempo*), cut into 1-in (2.5-cm) cubes
2 cups (500 ml) water
Cooking oil, as required
2 tablespoons minced garlic
½ cup (80 g) sliced red onion
2 tablespoons grated ginger
2 tablespoons fermented shrimp paste (*bagoong alamang*)
1 cup (250 ml) coconut cream
1 cup (250 ml) water
3–4 long green chilies (*siling mahaba*), thinly sliced
3–4 red bird's-eye chilies (*siling labuyo*), finely chopped
Salt and pepper, to taste
3–4 red bird's-eye chilies (*siling labuyo*), whole, to garnish

1. In a shallow skillet, boil the pork belly in the water until soft and the water has completely evaporated. When the pan is dry, add the cooking oil and let the meat crisp up until golden brown.
2. In the same pan, add the garlic, onion and ginger. Sauté until fragrant. Add the shrimp paste, coconut cream and water. Let it simmer for 5–10 minutes on medium heat.
3. Throw in most of the chilies (reserve a little green chilies for garnish) and simmer under low heat for another 15–20 minutes or so until the sauce thickens and the coconut cream has separated.
4. Season with salt and pepper and top with the remaining green chilies and whole red chilies. Serve with steaming rice.

# BEEF DISHES

Beef is another meat Filipinos love, but since it is pricier than pork, it is served less frequently in the Philippines though often served during special occasions. Again, Filipinos have been intrepid in drawing on its diverse culinary influences and indigenizing the use of beef in cooking. Bistek for example perfectly balances the savoriness of beef with salty soy sauce and sourness from local calamansi limes.

Although beef has found its way into more indigenous preparations like Filipino stew (*sinigang*), reflecting the historical availability of cattle in the Philippines, it is much more commonly found in dishes inspired by Spanish or American cooking. Salpicao, Caldereta or Picadillo all draw on the Spanish culinary influence in the Philippines, while Chili con carne uses ground or diced beef in a classic tex-mex style of cooking. And of course owing to the American presence, hamburgers and canned corned beef are wildly popular among Filipinos for their taste and convenience.

In most cases, goat, lamb or *caribou* meat can be substituted into most classic Filipino beef dishes depending on the region.

# Filipino Beefsteak Bistek Tagalog

Derived from the Spanish word *bistec*, Bistek Tagalog is the Filipino evolution of thinly sliced marinated beef steak. Traditional Bistek Tagalog is marinated in calamansi juice and soy sauce, pan fried and then smothered with either lightly cooked or raw onions, depending on the choice of the chef. Due to the relative simplicity and year round availability of the ingredients, it is a very popular dish in the Philippines. It's important to get your cooking oil very hot for the initial searing of the beef. I tend to cook the onions for an extended period favoring a tender caramelized finish which adds a hint of sweetness compared to having the onions raw or only lightly cooked. You can also add half your onion along with the beef, and the other half just for a minute or two at the end to have the best of both worlds.

**Good for 6–8**
**Prep time: 1 hour**
**Cooking time: 20 minutes**

½ cup (125 ml) water
½ cup (125 ml) calamansi juice
½ cup (125 ml) soy sauce
1 tablespoon ground black pepper
2 lbs (1 kg) beef tenderloin/breakfast
   steak, thinly sliced
Cooking oil, as needed
2–3 onions, sliced into rings
Salt and pepper, to taste

1. In a large mixing bowl, combine the water, calamansi juice, soy sauce and black pepper to make the marinade. Add the beef slices, stir until they are well-coated in the mixture. Let it marinate for at least 30 minutes to an hour—or overnight in the fridge for better flavor.
2. In a large, shallow skillet, heat up some cooking oil until it reaches smoke point.
3. Using tongs, take the beef slices from the marinade and place in the hot skillet. Reserve the marinade.
4. Sear the beef on high heat for about two minutes on each side.
5. Add the onions and cook for 2–3 minutes until translucent.
6. In the same skillet, pour in the reserved marinade. Let it simmer for 10 minutes to ensure the beef is tender and the marinade has reduced. Adjust the seasoning with salt and pepper to taste. Serve with steaming white rice.

# Fil-Mex Habanero Chili Con Carne

So while the mainstay chili of the Philippines is undisputedly the red bird's-eye *siling labuyo*, other types of chilies grow well in the Philippines, including the deadly bell-shaped habanero which reached the Philippines from Mexico in centuries past. I prefer to use habaneros for my Pinoy chili con carne in recognition of the Central American origins of this dish. I like my chili con carne to be chunky, so in addition to ground pork, I include some finely diced beef brisket—one of my favorite slow cook beef cuts with fantastic texture. A little citrus tang is great in chili con carne, and it can be balanced with almost any cheese, though I like to use local ingredients as much as possible, so when in the Philippines, I'll use calamansi and *kesong puti* (local water buffalo cheese). Plenty of fresh coriander leaves (cilantro) is a must and you can serve this with rice, tortillas or corn chips.

**Good for 6–8**
**Prep time: 20 minutes**
**Cooking time: 1 and a half hours**

Cooking oil, as required
1 large brown onion, diced
¼ cup (20g) finely chopped garlic
1 lb (500 g) ground pork
1 lb (500 g) beef brisket, diced
1 large carrot, chopped
1 large or 2 medium bell peppers, deseeded and diced
1 teaspoon ground cumin
1 teaspoon dried oregano
1 teaspoon ground paprika
1 teaspoon chili powder
2 fresh habanero chilies, finely chopped (if you like it really hot, add more habeneros with caution)
2 lbs (1 kg) fresh tomatoes (or 2 canned diced tomatoes)
1 cup (250 ml) beef stock (or equivalent organic beef stock powder)
1 can (10 oz/300 g) red kidney beans
1 can (10 oz/300 g) white cannellini beans
1 cob fresh corn (10 oz/300 g) or canned whole corn kernels can be substituted
7 oz (200 g) *kesong puti* or buffalo cheese (if unavailable try Monterey Jack or Colby), to garnish
1 bunch fresh coriander leaves (cilantro), to garnish
Cornflour tortillas or corn chips, to serve
10 calamansi limes (or 2 regular limes may be substituted), to serve

1. In a large cooking pot, heat up the oil and sauté the onion and garlic.
2. In the same pot, add the ground pork and cook until brown. Then add the diced beef, also cooking until browned.
3. Add the carrot and bell peppers and cook for 5 minutes.
4. Add the herbs and spices: cumin, oregano, paprika, chili powder and the diced habanero chilies and cook for two minutes
5. Add the fresh or canned tomatoes and beef stock. Mix well. Bring to a boil, then simmer on low heat for 45–60 minutes, or until the mixture has reduced and everything is well integrated.
6. Add the canned beans and corn kernels and mix well. Cook for a further five minutes.
7. Garnish with *kesong puti* and fresh coriander leaves. Serve with corn chips and calamansi limes on the side.

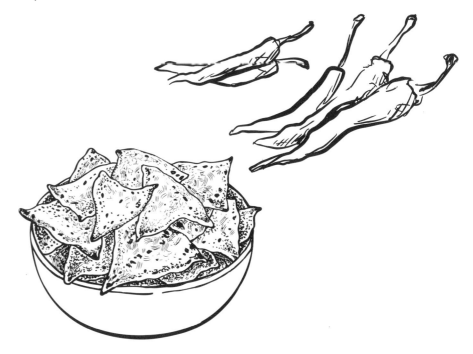

# "No Shortcut" Caldereta and Filipino "Calderetang Baka"

Caldereta, an iconic Filipino dish, symbolic of the adaptation of Spanish culinary styles in the Philippines—and yet for the longest time I loathed eating it—my experiences trying it in restaurants and street side *carinderias* was always the same—bland, boring, and that distinct drying out of the throat one gets from MSG-laden foods. This recipe has been a real victim of industrialized food preparation in the Philippines. It was only when I read the history of the dish that I was determined to cook it properly, with two rules—only fresh ingredients and NO shortcuts! While this takes a lot longer to cook the results are well worth it. Tender, falling apart cubes of beef, a thick, nourishing and rich flavored sauce are elevated by the addition of real dill pickles, salty black olives, and creamy homemade yogurt. Far from boring, when done properly, Caldereta is absolutely divine and bridges European, South American and Southeast Asian cooking. And the only trick is to go back to basics and cook it the way it was 300 years ago!

**Good for 6–8 persons**
**Prep time: 20–30 minutes**
**Cooking time: 2–3 hours**

Cooking oil, as required
¼ cup (20g) finely chopped garlic
1 medium red onion, chopped
1 medium white or brown onion, chopped
2 lbs (1 kg) beef—go for rump, round or brisket, cut into
    chunks or *caldereta* cut
2 medium carrots, chopped into ½-in (1-cm) semi-circles
2 medium potatoes, chopped into ¾-in (2-cm) chunks
2 medium bell peppers (ideally one red and one green)
1 cup (250 ml) dry red wine (try *tempranillo*, *sangiovese*,
    or a light bodied merlot)
2 lbs (1 kg) fresh tomatoes, diced
3 bay leaves
Salt and pepper, to season
10–15 whole green olives
3–4 medium dill pickles
2 tablespoons plain yogurt or sour cream
Fresh bell pepper, thinly sliced, to garnish

1. In a large cooking pot, heat the cooking oil and sauté the garlic and onion.

2. Once the onions are translucent, add the beef cubes and cook on high heat until it is browned on all sides.

3. Add the carrots and cook for 2–3 minutes.

4. Add the potatoes, bell peppers, red wine, diced tomatoes, bay leaves and season with salt and pepper. Slow cook the stew for 2–3 hours over low heat.

5. Once the meat is soft and tender and the mixture has reduced to a thick, hearty stew, add the olives and sliced dill pickles.

6. Stir through the yogurt or sour cream to get a thick, rich consistency. Let it simmer for 2 minutes and serve with steaming hot rice. Garnish with thin slices of bell pepper. You can pair it with the same wine used in cooking—if there is any left!

# Pinoy Picadillo With Banana Chips

Picadillo is another Spanish-Mexican influenced dish that has been adapted to the Philippines culinary landscape over the years. While Latin American picadillo usually contains hints of sweet and sour from raisins and capers respectively, the Philippine adaptation—perhaps reflecting the limited availability of those ingredients during the colonial period—is a more savory/salty dish, with just a little sweetness coming from the use of carrots and peas in the dish. Filipinos also tend to add substance, serving it with hard boiled quail eggs. This is a dish that is easy to experiment based on whatever you have in the pantry—try sneaking in a few crispy banana chips.  The best part about is perhaps the leftovers—you can use them as an impromptu filling for *tortang talong*, or *empanadas*!

**Good for 6–8**
**Prep time: 10 minutes**
**Cooking time: 25 minutes**

2 tablespoons cooking oil
2 tablespoons chopped garlic
1 onion, chopped
1 tomato, chopped
1 lb (500 g) ground beef
2 tablespoons tomato paste
2 bay leaves
1 potato, diced
1 carrot, diced
1½ cups (375 ml) beef broth or water
¼ cup (60 ml) fish sauce (*patis*)
¼ cup (30 g) green peas
12 hard boiled quail eggs
Salt and pepper, to taste
Onion leeks, to garnish
Parsley, to garnish
3 oz (50 g) banana chips, to garnish

1. In a shallow skillet, heat the oil and sauté the garlic, onion and tomato until fragrant. Add the ground beef and cook until brown.
2. Add the tomato paste, bay leaves, diced potatoes and carrots. Pour in the beef broth or water and fish sauce and simmer for 10 minutes.
3. Add the green peas and quail eggs and simmer for another 5 minutes.
4. Season with salt and pepper to desired taste. Serve hot with cooked rice. Garnish with a little onion leeks or parsley if you have some on hand, and of course some banana chips. If you don't have any dried banana chips, lightly fry some slices of plantain or any other bananas you have on hand—it really makes the dish!

# Chris Urbano's Fil-Am Corned Beef Sliders

Here's another recipe I developed for my show and blog *Maputing Cooking*. The idea was to come up with the perfect Filipino-American slider, which not only represented both cuisines, but showcased the Philippines' penchant for balancing contrasting flavors. While fresh ground chuck is the mainstay of the American burger pattie, beef in the Philippines is far more often eaten from tins—and corned beef *pan de sal* is one of the all time favorite—so this was the obvious base for the recipe. To this, we get our sweetness from caramelized onion, and a little relish or chutney, and our sourness from real dill pickles and some ballpark mustard. A piece of Monteray jack for creaminess and salt and a few chili leaves for a hint of bitterness. If you plan ahead, slow cooking the corned beef overnight in a can of local beer is the ultimate infusion of flavor, or you can enjoy a glass with these delicious sliders.

**Good for 6 as a snack/tapas**
**Prep time: 10 minutes**
**Cooking time: 20 minutes**

Cooking oil, as required
5 cloves garlic, diced
1 medium red onion, chopped
2 teaspoons brown sugar
1 can (10 oz/300 g) good quality canned
  corned beef
12 buns toasted *pan de sal*
1 bunch chili leaves (*dahon ng sili*)
½ lb (250 g) Colby Jack cheese (or similar)
2 tomatoes, sliced into circles
3 pcs dill pickles, sliced thinly
3 tablespoons mild "ballpark" mustard
3 tablespoons tomato ketchup

**1.** In a shallow skillet, heat the oil and sauté the garlic and onion. Add the brown sugar and cook until the onion is caramelized.

**2.** Add the corned beef and fry for five minutes, until the liquids have reduced. Set aside.

**3.** Slice the *pan de sal* into halves. In a large, shallow skillet, put a good amount of cooking oil and heat. Place the *pan de sal* halves in the hot oil, inner sides down. Fry for around 2 minutes, until they have absorbed the oil and are a crispy, golden brown. Then turn them over on the now dry fry pan and dry toast the exterior of the *pan de sal*. The goal is the interior fried/crunchy and the exterior, lightly toasted, but dry and non-oily

**4.** Grab the *pan de sal* "bottom" halves and arrange on a large chopping board. On each base, place 4 chili leaves, then a tablespoon of the corned beef mixture. Place a slice of Colby Jack cheese on top, it should melt slightly on the warm corned beef. Add a slice of tomato and a slice of pickle.

**5.** Next, spread just a little ballpark mustard and tomato ketchup on the inner side of the *pan de sal* top halves and place these on top to complete the slider.

**6.** Use Filipino and American flag toothpicks to fix the slider and serve with a cold beer.

# Beef Tapa Breakfast Burrito

Australians love their indulgent café breakfasts, but we don't always have time for a sit down breakfast. As such, "breakkie rolls" are now a popular takeaway option across Australia. Similar to the concept of a breakfast burrito in the United States—the idea is get what is essentially a full café breakfast, into something readily consumed with one hand! While Aussies will normally go for a bread roll or panini—I lean towards using a cornflour tortilla for my Pinoy-inspired Tapa Breakfast Burrito. A little buffalo cheese, avocado, watercress and chutney, breathe new life to the classic *tapsilog* flavor combination. Just roll everything in the tortilla and you're good to go!

**Good for 4 pieces**
**Prep time: 10 minutes**
**Cooking time: 20 minutes/2 minutes reheating**

1 lb (500 g) beef sirloin, thinly sliced
10 cloves garlic, diced
½ cup (125 ml) soy sauce
½ cup (125 ml) cane vinegar
2 tablespoons brown sugar
Salt and pepper, to taste
2–4 red bird's-eye chilies (*siling labuyo*), bruised
Olive oil, as required
4 tortilla wrappers, medium size
4 eggs
Salt and pepper, to season
2 tomatoes, sliced
1 avocado, sliced thinly
Fresh watercress or chili leaves
4 tablespoons fresh yogurt
4 teaspoons tomato chutney or relish
4 fresh calamansi limes (regular lime may be substituted)

1. Marinate the beef in the garlic, soy sauce, vinegar, sugar, salt, pepper and chilies. Mix well and leave for 30 minutes. For best results, marinate overnight.
2. Heat the oil and fry the beef slices in a shallow skillet until cooked through and the marinade is cooked off. Set aside.
3. Warm the tortillas on low heat in an oven, or microwave or in a skillet.
4. Crack a single egg in a small fry pan with a little olive oil. Quickly scramble it and season with salt and pepper, cook on one side only until it is just cooked through.
5. Lay a single tortilla on a chopping board. Place the thin cooked disc of scrambled egg on the tortilla.
6. Place two or three pieces of beef slices on top of the eggs, followed by two or three slices each of tomato and avocado. Place a little watercress, or a stem of chili leaves.
7. Top with 1 tablespoon of yogurt and 1 teaspoon of relish. Using a small strainer, squeeze a fresh calamansi or a lime wedge over the top.
8. Roll the tortilla as you would for a burrito. Tuck one end in and leaving the other end open. Roll in parchment paper and twist the ends to hold the burrito in shape when eating.

1. Warm the tortilla on low heat.

2. Place the thin cooked disc of scrambled egg on the tortilla.

3. Place 2–3 beef slices, 2–3 slices tomato and avocado, some watercress and a stem of chili leaves.

4. Top with 1 teaspoon yogurt and 1 tea-spoon relish.

5. Squeeze a fresh calamansi over the top.

6. Tuck one end in and leave the other end open, and roll in parchment paper.

7. Roll the tortilla as you would do for a burrito.

8. Twist the ends to hold the burrito in shape when eating.

# DESSERTS AND DRINKS

The Filipino palate loves extremes of flavor—and just as they can devour salty pork dish, or an eye-wateringly sour stew (*sinigang*), they love sweets and sugary treats just as much. The love for sugar can be seen in the desserts Filipinos love, which showcase a myriad of culinary influences over the centuries. There's the Spanish influence through the flans, cremes and meringues; Filipino *leche flan* is world class and one of my all time favorites. The American influence popularized pies, cakes, ice creams and jelly. While sugar, eggs and flour have become the basis for Filipino desserts nothing beats the traditional desserts *kakanin* or sticky rice cakes made with local starchy ingredients like *malagkit* (glutinous rice) and cassava flour and grated coconut (*niyog*). Suman, Biko, Bibingka, Puto, Sapin-sapin, Kutsinta, Palitaw and Pichi-pichi are some popular *kakanin*. They are steamed, boiled or baked and most are wrapped in banana leaves. These are often served with freshly grated coconut and muscovado sugar or white sugar. In recent years chefs have experimented with more complex variants, such as serving Puto or Pichi-pichi with cheese for a salty/sweet kick. The Mexican inspired Champorado combines cocoa with dried fish to give a salted chocolate taste in this wildly popular "frankenfood".

If there's one dessert that truly demonstrates the global nature of Filipino food, it is the *halo-halo*. Known as the Queen of Filipino desserts and by literal definition meaning "mix-mix", this is remarkable in its complexity and juxtaposition of ingredients, but when eaten simply tastes balanced and "meant to be". Although Indonesia and Malaysia also lay claim to a shaved ice mixed fruit based dessert, what elevates *halo-halo* is the incorporation of Spanish and American ingredients, such as *leche flan*, jello and sweet corn with the indigenous flavors of purple yam (*ube*), sago, coconut and beans.

In the tropical heat and humidity of the Philippines, drinks are usually of the iced variety and an abundance of fruity concoctions awaits anybody who needs to quench their thirst. With the abundance of delicious tropical fruits in the Philippines, one is spoilt for choice, whether it be fresh pineapple juice which aids in digestion, or refreshing calamansi juice sweetened with a hint of sugar or honey. Samalamig or the fruit-flavored water and Sago't Gulaman are the common man's thirst quencher. With a stick of barbecue or *isaw*, this is a perfect pair.

Mango or banana shakes are widely available, but almost any fruit in season can be blended over ice, even the pungent durian. My favorite Filipino fruit shake to make at home combines fresh papaya, Lacatan bananas, with *carabao* yogurt, local honey and a hint of calamansi lime for a kick.

During evenings and cooler weather, hot ginger tea or *salabat* is popular and believed to cure colds and sore throat. While on special occasions like Christmas eve, hot chocolate made from homegrown *tablea* is a favorite. While not known as a coffee producing country, the Philippine's local coffee is a robust brew known as *barako* (Liberica), although *kopi luwak* or coffee sourced from the excrement of civet cats can also be found here.

Though my favorite way to refresh in the Philippines is with a chilled fresh *buko* or young coconut, the taste of a freshly picked coconut is really something special and the perfect way to rehydrate after days of trekking or island hopping in this beautiful archipelago.

# Creamy Fruit Salad

In every gathering and fiesta that you will be invited to, it is normal to always see a colorful cream filled bowl of fruit salad served for dessert. In the Philippines, cans of fruit cocktail are often used for convenience—but whether you like to use fresh or canned fruits, or a combination of both, there are no hard rules what can go in—though you normally want a minimum of at least four ingredients plus the coconut. Accordingly, my fruit salad may be different each time depending on where I am, and what season it is—though I do like to add at least one tin of canned fruit along with a little of the syrup for extra sweetness. Filipinos will sometimes grate in a mild cheddar cheese which adds a salty kick and is worth trying out—though I prefer to keep mine to just the fruits. Garnish with fresh mint leaves before serving.

**Good for 6–8**
**Prep time: 10 minutes/4 hours chilling time**
**Cooking time: No cooking needed**

3 cups (530 g) whipped cream
1 cup (250 ml) condensed milk
1 cup (175 g) young coconut (*buko*) meat, shredded
2 cups (350 g) melon, cut into cubes
2 cups (350 g) ripe mango, cut into cubes
1 cup (175 g) green and red apples, skin intact and cut into cubes
1 cup (175 g) red/green grapes, cut in half
1 cup (175 g) strawberries, cut in half
1 cup (175 g) kiwi, sliced into half moon
1 cup (175 g) pineapple, cut into chunks
Mint leaves, chopped, for garnish

1. In a large mixing bowl, whip the cream with an electric mixer on a moderate setting or a manual whisk until it becomes stiff. Gently fold in the condensed milk while whipping the cream.
2. Add all the fruits to the bowl and mix everything well. Cover or transfer to a large food storage container with an airtight lid and store it in the fridge for 2–4 hours or until chilled.
3. Transfer to small bowls and top with chopped mint leaves when serving.

# Lime and Vanilla Leche Flan

*Leche flan* is perhaps the most recognizable of Filipino desserts after *halo-halo* and is a delicious note to end any meal on. Literally meaning "milk flan", the recipe combines condensed milk, with egg yolks to create a luscious, melt in the mouth dessert. While buying leche flan is easy—its available at every market around the Philippines—this really benefit from the time and patience required of home cooking. To get the best results, it's essential to twice-strain the milk-yolk mixture slowly through a cheese cloth, which results in an immaculately smooth texture. Also, home cooking allows an opportunity to infuse the *leche flan* with other flavors. I heat the milk with rosemary sprigs, vanilla pod, and some calamansi zest prior to using—simple to do, these little tweaks add enormous flavor and will be sure to impress.

**Good for 6–8 as dessert**
**Prep time: 20 minutes**
**Cooking time: 45 minutes to 1 hour/1–2 hours cooling time**

1 cup (250 ml) condensed cream or milk
1 cup (250 ml) fresh milk
Hint of vanilla essence
2–3 rosemary sprigs
½ teaspoon calamansi zest, for the infusion
10 egg yolks
1 cup (200 g) sugar
2 tablespoons sugar per *llanera*
Additional sugar for the caramel topping, you need (about 2 tablespoons sugar per llanera
*Llanera* (a small, oval shaped aluminum tin—used specifically for *leche flan*, as it heats quickly and evenly to caramelize the sugar)

1. In a pot, make the *leche flan* mixture by combining the condensed cream/milk, fresh milk, vanilla essence, rosemary sprigs and calamansi zest. Simmer the mixture for twenty minutes at a very low heat. Turn off the heat just before the mixture starts to boil.
2. Using a strainer, transfer the rosemary and calamansi-infused *leche flan* mixture to another bowl to strain out the rosemary sprigs.
3. In another large bowl, combine the egg yolks and sugar. Mix it with the strained *leche flan* mixture. Stir until well-combined.
4. Use a cheesecloth to strain the mixture. Strain it twice to ensure that all the big particles are removed and a smooth liquid is retained. This step is essential to ensure a very fine, smooth finish.
5. Put 2 tablespoons of sugar to a llanera and put it directly on low heat to make the caramel. Use tongs in holding the llanera to keep your hands from getting burned. Once the sugar turns amber, take it away from the heat. The darker the color gets, the more bitter the caramel—so take care not to overcook.
6. Pour the *leche flan* mixture to the *llanera* and cover it with foil.
7. Place it in the oven and bake in a water bath at 350°F (180°C). Cook for around 45 minutes or until the *leche flan* is cooked. Alternatively, you can also cook it by steaming. Prepare a steamer and put the *leche flan* inside. Steam for 45 minutes. With steaming be sure to check once or twice to ensure you do not run out of water. The *leche flan* is ready when you can insert a toothpick and it comes out clean.
8. Refrigerate the *leche flan* to cool it for 1–2 hours. Once cooled, take it out and serve. Try pairing it with a rich dessert wine like muscat.

# Filipino Chocolate Rice Porridge
## Champorado At Tuyo

It is believed that Champorado traces its origins to Mexico, though it has been adapted and localized in the Philippines. Champorado is a thick, slightly sweet rice porridge, flavored with cocoa. The dish uses sticky, glutinous rice and native cocoa and cooked to a very thick, almost pudding like consistency. Filipinos pair champorado with dried, salty fish (*tuyo*), this delights the Filipinos and repulses foreigners. Having tried this, it's much like enjoying salted chocolate, and the slight fishy flavor surprisingly just seems to work. In my version, I like to take a shortcut by stirring through a few pieces of high grade dark chocolate into my sweetened glutinous rice (*malagkit*), and topping some milk for a creamier porridge. I add *cacao* nibs for a bit of nuttiness and texture. It's a great dish for newcomers to Filipino food, showcasing the cuisine's tendency to integrate strong opposing flavors in a single dish.

**Good for 6–8**
**Prep time: 5 minutes**
**Cooking time: 30 minutes**

3 cups (750 ml) water
½ cup (100 g) brown sugar
1½ cups (300 g) uncooked glutinous rice (*malagkit*)
1¼ cups (200 g) native chocolate *tablea* or dark chocolate (it should be >60% cocoa solids)
½ cup (125 ml) fresh milk or pouring cream
2–3 oz (50–75 g) Cacao nibs, (optional)—to serve
3–4 pieces (about ½ lb/250 g) *tuyo* (or any available salted/dried fish, optional), to serve

1. In a cooking pot, add the water and brown sugar and bring to a boil.
2. Rinse and then add the glutinous rice and let it cook for 30 minutes or until cooked, stirring from time to time with a wooden spoon or spatula to avoid it sticking to the bottom.
3. Once the rice is cooked to a thick, porridge-like consistency, add the dark chocolate and let it melt and blend in with the *champorado*.
4. When serving, drizzle a little milk/pouring cream over each bowl, a sprinkle of cacao nibs and serve with *tuyo* (salted dried fish).

# Fresh Fruit and Preserved Mixed Ice Dessert Halo-Halo

Halo-halo is the iconic Filipino dessert, and probably the best metaphor for explaining what Filipino food is. Literally meaning "mix-mix," it is a combination of sweet and preserved fruits, legumes, corn, gelatin cubes, yam and *leche flan*, topped with shaved ice and milk. You can see a little of every culinary influence in this technicolor and cool dessert. Halo-halo is eaten everywhere in the Philippines, and a popular *merienda* or afternoon treat. While on the surface it closely resembles the *es buah*, or *es campur* found in Indonesia and Malaysia respectively, halo-halo is a lot more interesting as it combines indigenous, Asian and Western ingredients. My take on this classic is inspired by eating Indonesia's *es buah* and its use of more fresh fruits. I like the textural combination of perfectly ripened fresh fruits, along with the preserved ones. I've added Indonesian influence to the mix—or more "halo" to my halo-halo!

**Good for 6–8**
**Prep time: 20 minutes**
**Cooking time: No cooking needed**

1 cup (175 g) sliced banana
1 cup (175 g) diced jackfruit (*langka*)
2 cups (350 g) cubed avocado
2 cups (350 g) cubed mango
2 cups (350 g) cubed ripe papaya
1 cup (175 g) diced young coconut (*buko*) meat
1 cup (175 g) canned sweet corn kernels
1 cup (175 g) sweet white beans or red/green mung beans
1 cup (175 g) sweetened purple yam (*ube*) jam
1 *leche flan* (page 129)
1 cup (250 ml) sweetened condensed milk
Shaved/crushed ice, as needed

**1.** Make the *leche flan* by following the recipe on page 129.
**2.** Prepare the ingredients in separate medium-sized bowls or jars and line them up.
**3.** In a tall glass or a medium-sized bowl, put 1–2 tablespoons of each ingredient. Add shaved ice on top until it reaches the glass' mouth. Finish it up with a spoonful of *ube* jam and a piece of leche flan. Scoop 2–3 tablespoons of condensed milk on top or until you get the desired sweetness.
**4.** With a dessert spoon, stir everything together and enjoy while cold.
**5.** Remember—with *halo-halo*, there are literally no rules what can go in, so if you're missing one or two things, or add others, that's totally fine—and very Filipino! Only the shaved ice, the condensed milk and having a minimum of six things of different colors or textures in your *halo-halo* is compulsory.

# Banana And Jackfruit Sweet Rolls
## Turon

Turon is a plantain banana dessert. The banana is rolled in brown sugar and wrapped in spring roll wrapper before frying. This is a favorite afternoon snack in the Philippines, and you will definitely see street vendor on nearly every block in Manila selling this. I like to jazz this up in dinner parties by serving it with purple yam, vanilla ice cream and mint. It's also great to add other fruits inside the turon. Shreds of jackfruit (*langka*) are commonly used alongside the plantain banana, though if you don't have any available I'll often use a second, sweeter type of banana, like *lacatan*, or *senoritas*. Slices of fresh strawberry works well too.

**Good for 6–8 as snack/dessert**
**Prep time: 20 minutes**
**Cooking time: 30 minutes**

20 *lumpia* wrappers (ordinary Chinese spring roll wrappers may be substituted)
10 *saba* bananas, sliced in half lengthwise
½ cup (50 g) brown sugar
½ cup (90 g) sliced jackfruit (*langka*), (optional)
½ cup (90 g) sliced fresh strawberry, (optional)
Cooking oil, for frying
Vanilla ice cream and purple yam (*ube*) jam, to serve

1. In a clean space or a large plate, place one *lumpia* wrapper. Take a slice of banana and roll it in the brown sugar. Place it about ⅓ of the way up the *lumpia* wrapper.
2. Add some sliced jackfruit or strawberries parallel to the piece of banana.
3. Fold the *lumpia* wrapper over the fruit and pull it back towards you, tightening and compacting the fruit inside. Fold the ends in and roll the rest of the *turon*, as you would an ordinary spring roll. Using your finger, dab a little water as required to help seal the *turon*.
4. Once you've rolled all the *turon*, sprinkle 2 tablespoons of brown sugar over the top of them.
5. In a shallow fry pan, add about half an inch of cooking oil and heat to 350°F (180°C).
6. Shallow fry the *turon* for 5–7 minutes on medium heat, turning as required until all sides are golden brown. Remove from the pan and place on paper towels, or a wire rack to drain excess oil.
7. Serve on a plate with vanilla ice cream and *ube* jam on top.

# Brown Sugar Sticky Rice Cakes with Coconut Biko

Kakanin or rice cakes are very popular *merienda* snacks for the Filipinos—and *biko* has long been my favorite. I like the rich molasses notes from brown sugar, while the crispy, sweet granules of latik (a crumbly residue derived from long simmering of coconut cream) is divine. In the Philippines, *biko* is normally set on a circular woven dish known as a *bilao*, lined with banana leaf that has been gently toasted over fire. While it adds aroma and authenticity, if you don't have these handy don't let it stop you plating some delicious *biko* using a pizza tray and some baking paper. *Biko* is extremely filling, so this dish will go a long way and one or two small pieces will be sure to satisfy your afternoon hunger pangs!

2 cups (400 g) uncooked glutinous rice
2 cups (500 ml) coconut cream (*kakang gata*)
2 cups (500 ml) water
1½ cups (210 g) palm sugar (*panutsa*)
1 cup (210 g) brown sugar
Pinch of salt
*Bilao*/Banana leaves (optional)

**LATIK**
2 cups (500 ml) coconut cream

**Good for 6–8 as snack/*merienda***
**Prep time: 20 minutes**
**Cooking time: 30 minutes**

1. Make the Latik by pouring the coconut cream into a skillet and bring it to a boil. Continuously stir until the cream separates the oil and curds. Let the curds wither and then toast in their own oil. Remove the now crispy-fried curds and place on paper towels to drain excess oil.
2. Wash the rice and transfer it to a pot. Mix in the coconut cream and water and let it boil. Stir constantly to avoid sticking.
3. Once the rice is almost done, add the palm sugar, brown sugar and salt. Stir until well mixed. Add the rest of the water if the mixture is too thick. The final consistency should be thick enough to hold its shape when spread over the *bilao*.
4. Cut a circular piece of banana leaf the same size as the *bilao* to be used. Run the banana leaf over the fire quickly till it takes on a glossy sheen. Gas stove burners, or a kitchen blow torch can both be used to safely do this at home. (If you do not have banana leaves, simply line a baking tray with baking paper instead).
5. Place the circle onto the *bilao*. Transfer the rice into the *bilao* and flatten. Top with the Latik. Allow to cool in a cool dry location—and enjoy!

# Ginger and Coconut Rice Cakes with Mango Suman

Another of the rice cakes that is easy to prepare at home is *suman*. What makes this rice cake different is it is flavored with ginger, white sugar, and adopts some herbaceous notes from being steamed in a banana leaf. Suman is quite subtle in its flavor among all the Filipino *kakanin*, and for this reason, it is usually partnered with fresh mango, and hot chocolate. This is a fascinating pairing—as the combination of sticky rice and ripe mango is practiced in Malaysia, whereas hot chocolate has Central American origins—another example of the global fusion found in Filipino food. Enjoy this delight, one starts with a bite of fresh mango, then a bite of *suman*, usually dipped in a little more raw sugar, and then you chase it down with the hot cocoa. Its hard to compare—but the effect is a bit like eating orange infused dark chocolate. Global flavors, uniquely Filipino, utterly delicious and sure to impress your friends!

**Good for 6–8**
**Prep time: 20 minutes**
**Cooking time: 30 minutes**

2 cups (400 g) uncooked glutinous rice (*malagkit*), washed and soak in water for 20 minutes, drained
2 cups (500 ml) coconut cream
2 tablespoons grated ginger
Pinch of salt
2 cups (420 g) sugar
Banana leaf
¼ cup (50 g) muscovado sugar, to serve
½ fresh mango, to serve
Hot chocolate, to serve

1. Pour the coconut cream, ginger, salt and sugar into a pot. Add the rice and let it cook half way. Add some water if the mixture is too thick. Set aside and let it cool.
2. Run the banana leaf over the fire once and cut into squares around 8 in by 8 in (20 x 20 cm).
3. Place the square banana leaf in front of you and tilt it 45 degrees, so you have a diamond shape in front of you. To wrap the *suman*, place 2–3 tablespoons of the rice at about ⅓ of the way up the diamond in a horizontal line. Fold the near point of the banana leaf over the rice and pull it back to pack the rice into a tighter log. Roll the *suman* in the remaining banana leaf folding in the left and right points of the square at the halfway point.
4. Cut some thin strips of banana leaf, about ½ in (1 cm) wide. Hold two *suman* together and tie each end with a banana leaf strip to hold them together and prevent the leaf from unrolling.
5. Gather the *suman* and place in a steamer. Steam for about 40 minutes until the *suman* is fully cooked.
6. Serve with sugar, fresh mango and hot chocolate.

# Filipino Style Fruit Punch

This is a refreshing treat served at any large Filipino gathering or celebration. Cool and fruity, its perfect in the tropical heat and popular with children and adults alike. When making this in the Philippines, I like to juice a fresh pineapple myself, and home make the ginger syrup, but in a pinch, canned pineapple juice and fizzy ginger ale are perfectly adequate. I like adding some fresh rambutans to my punch if they're in season, as an extra fruity surprise in the mix. Often at Filipino parties, the punch will be supplemented with gin or vodka as a party starter once the kids have gone to bed.

**Makes 8–12 cups (2–3 l)**
**Prep time: 10 minutes**
**Cooking time: 5 minutes (if making ginger syrup)**

4 cups (1 l) unsweetened pineapple juice
4 cups (1 l) orange juice
1¼ cups (320 ml) soda water or lemonade
1 cup (120 g) orange, sliced into rings
1 cup (120 g) calamansi limes, sliced into rings
   (regular limes may be substituted)
1 cup (120 g) red apples, cubed
15 pcs fresh rambutans, peeled (or 1 cup/250 g
   preserved canned lychees may be substitured)

**GINGER SYRUP**
½ cup (125 ml) water
¼ cup (50 g) sugar
4 in (10 cm) ginger root, smashed

**1.** To make the Ginger Syrup, put the water, sugar and pounded ginger in a small pot. Allow to boil for 5 minutes or until the sugar is dissolved. Use a strainer to remove the pounded ginger and set the liquid aside to cool down.
**2.** In a pitcher or punch bowl, combine the pineapple juice, orange juice, soda water or lemonade and Ginger Syrup and mix well.
**3.** Add the sliced citrus, apples, lychees and peeled rambutans (if using).
**4.** Allow to cool in the fridge for 15 minutes. Add ice cubes when serving to keep the punch cold for longer.

# Lemon-Lime Mint Julep

A great way to beat the tropical heat in the Philippines—the julep has
been a popular cocktail in Manila for decades and is simple to make.
You can try this with native calamansi, though I prefer the classic
combination of lemon with whiskey.

**Makes 4 glasses**
**Prep time: 15 minutes**
**Cooking time: No cooking needed**

1 cup (25 g) fresh mint leaves
¼ cup (50 g) sugar
1 cup (250 ml) lemon-lime soda
½ cup (125 ml) whiskey (scotch,
　bourbon or local Philippine whiskey
　can be used)
1 teaspoon vanilla essence
¼ cup (60 ml) freshly squeezed lemon
　juice
Crushed ice, as needed
Fresh mint leaves, to garnish
Lemon wedges, to garnish

**1.** Place the mint leaves in a pitcher and
muddle with a wooden spoon until wilted. Add
the sugar.
**2.** Pour in the soda, whiskey, vanilla essence
and fresh lemon juice. With a stirrer, mix
everything together.
**3.** Serve in glasses with crushed iced,
garnished with fresh mint leaves and lemon
wedges.

# Mango Shakes

This is the iconic poolside companion at resorts around the Philippines, drawing on the world class mangoes that grow all over the country. I like a thinner mango shake, and use coconut water to extend it a little, though you can make a creamier shake by using fresh milk, or coconut milk instead. Green mango shake is a nice variant to try, just add more honey, or a little sugar until the right balance of sweet/sour is achieved.

**Makes 2 glasses**
**Prep time: 10 minutes**
**Cooking time: No cooking time**

3 medium sized ripe mangoes (or green mangoes)
1 tablespoon honey
½ cup (100 g) raw sugar (if using green mangoes)
2 cups (500 ml) fresh *buko* juice (coconut water)
Crushed ice, as needed
Fresh mint leaves, to garnish

1. Slice open the mango and remove the soft flesh using a spoon. For green mangoes, use a vegetable peeler to remove the skin and then slice off the mango cheeks, cutting into a few smaller pieces.
2. In a blender, add the mangoes together with the honey or sugar, coconut water and about 10 mint leaves.
3. Add the ice and blend until smooth with no mango chunks left.
4. Pour in tall glasses, add bendable straws and serve. Garnish with mint leaves.

# Sago Pandan Cooler Sago't Gulaman

Known as a *palamig*—iterally something that "cools", Sago't Gulaman is a refreshment found widely on the streets of the Philippines. It resembles a sort of improvised native cordial, using brown sugar, pandan leaves and either banana or vanilla essence to flavor ice cold water. Usually tapioca pearls (sago) and cubes of gelatin are added for color and texture.

**Makes 6 glasses**
**Prep time: 10 minutes**
**Cooking time: 10 minutes**

3 cups (750 ml) water
5 pieces pandan leaves
1 cup (200 g) brown sugar
1 cup (240 g) green unflavored gelatin, cooked according to package, cut into cubes
1 cup (240 g) red unflavored gelatin, cooked according to package, cut into cubes
1½ cups (350 g) large sago (tapioca) pearls, cooked according to package
1 teaspoon banana essence
Crushed ice, as needed

1. Combine the water, pandan leaves and brown sugar in a pot to cook the syrup.

2. Bring it to a boil for about 5 minutes until all the sugar is completely dissolved. Let the pandan leaves steep until the syrup cools down. Remove the pandan leaves.

3. Get a water pitcher add the gelatin cubes and sago pearls. Pour the sugar syrup.

4. Add the banana essence and mix everything.

5. Adjust the taste base on your preference. You can add more sugar if you want it to be sweeter. Serve in tall glasses with ice.

6 Scoop and distribute the ingredients in each glass before serving.

# Filipino Sangria

My family worked in the wine industry in Australia, so I grew up with a passion for wine at a young age. Today, I've been sharing with fans of *Maputing Cooking* how to incorporate wine into Filipino cuisine. And with sangria being a cold, wine based punch—I find this perfectly suited to Philippines' hot tropical climate. While there are many ways to prepare sangria, I created something "by Filipinos, for Filipinos" with this recipe. I use a very light colored rose wine, made using the sangiovese grape varietal, and flavor it with *dalandan* (a local Philippine orange) and calamansi. Sangiovese is known for strawberry notes, and these grow well in Baguio, so I pop in a few of those. A sprig or two of fresh tarragon will really make this "pop" in your mouth. If you can't find a sangiovese rose, opt for any lighter bodied red wine like pinot noir.

**Makes 4 cups (1 l)**
**Prep time: 10 minutes**
**Cooking time: No cooking needed**

¼ cup (50 g) raw sugar
½ cup (125 ml) boiling water
1 bottle red wine (a Sangiovese Rose or any light bodied red wine)
¼ cup (60 ml) triple sec (optional)
1 orange, sliced into rings
1 *dalandan*, sliced into rings
10–15 calamansi limes, sliced into halves
1 cup (120 g) strawberries, sliced into halves
2–3 sprigs tarragon
1 can (10 oz/330ml) soda water
1 can (10 oz/330ml) lemonade
Ice cubes, as needed

1. Make a simple sugar syrup by combining the raw sugar with the boiling water in a cup and stir until the sugar dissolves.
2. In a pitcher, combine the wine, triple sec, sugar syrup, citrus fruits and strawberries and mix using a stirrer.
3. Gently bruise two sprigs of tarragon and place in the sangria.
4. Top it off with the can of soda water for some fizz and some of the lemonade. Taste the sangria and add more lemonade for a sweeter taste, depending on your palate.
5. Keep in the fridge for 15 minutes to allow the fruit flavors to infuse. Add ice cubes when serving to keep it cool.

# Lemongrass Iced Tea

Lemongrass is a popular addition in Filipino cook and very easy to grow in pots at home. I love the flavor it imparts in drinks though and this lemongrass ice tea is no exception. A lot of ice tea these days is made from cheap powder mixes which predominantly comprise sugar. Your taste buds will be delighted using real brewed tea, herbs and adding the right amount of sugar for your palate and to ensure it's not too sickly sweet.

**Makes 8 cups (2 l)**
**Prep time: 10 minutes**
**Cooking time: 5 minutes**

3 stems lemongrass bulb, pounded and
   chopped
½ cup (100 g) raw sugar
4 cups (1 l) water
1 cup (250 ml) calamansi/lemon Juice
2 cups (500 ml) brewed tea (tea bags/
   leaves removed), cooled to room
   temperature
Ice cubes, as needed
4–6 lemongrass stems, to serve
¼ cup (60 ml) thinly sliced calamansi
   limes/lemon
Mint leaves, to garnish

1. In a deep pot, mix the lemongrass, sugar and 2 cups of water and boil for 5 minutes or until the sugar is completely dissolved. Let the drink steep in the lemongrass' flavor to get a rich lemongrass syrup until it cools down. Use a strainer to remove the lemongrass and other impurities. Set aside.
2. In a pitcher, mix the lemongrass syrup and calamansi/lime juice and brewed tea. Add the remaining 2 cups of water. Taste the mixture and add more water if it's too sweet.
3. In a highball glass, place some ice cubes, a whole lemongrass stem and some sliced calamansi or lemon. Then fill the glass with ice tea, garnish with the mint leaves and serve ice cold.

# Papaya Banana Lime Smoothie

This is my favorite shake to make at home in the Philippines, and one I love to have mid-morning after exercise. Banana and papaya are both cheap and plentiful in the Philippines. In Australia, papaya or the sub-tropical pawpaw are usually served with a squeeze of lime, which really makes the flavors of the fruit come to life and adds a real "zing" in the mouth. Add a tablespoon or two of muesli, and you'll have a healthy breakfast to start the day!

**Makes 2 glasses**
**Prep time: 10 minutes**
**Cooking time: No cooking needed**

2 medium bananas, peeled
¼ medium ripe papaya (cut in cubes)
¼ cup (60 ml) calamansi juice
1 tablespoon honey
1 cup (250 ml) unsweetened/greek
   yogurt
1 cup (250 ml) milk (use water for a
   lighter shake)
Ice cubes, as needed

1. Combine the peeled bananas, papaya, calamansi juice, honey, yogurt and milk in a blender, or a suitable jug if using a stick blender.
2. Blend everything until smooth and creamy and there are no papaya and banana chunks left.
3. Pour into a glass over a few ice cubes (if you like it cold) and serve.

# INDEX

Published by Tuttle Publishing, an imprint of
Periplus Editions (HK) Ltd

www.tuttlepublishing.com

Library of Congress Control Number: 2018943058

ISBN 978-0-8048-4925-8

Distributed by

*North America, Latin America & Europe*
Tuttle Publishing
364 Innovation Drive
North Clarendon, VT 05759-9436 U.S.A.
Tel: 1 (802) 773-8930; Fax: 1 (802) 773-6993
info@tuttlepublishing.com; www.tuttlepublishing.com

*Japan*
Tuttle Publishing
Yaekari Building 3rd Floor
5-4-12 Osaki
Shinagawa-ku
Tokyo 141-0032
Tel: (81) 3 5437-0171; Fax: (81) 3 5437-0755
sales@tuttle.co.jp; www.tuttle.co.jp

*Asia Pacific*
Berkeley Books Pte. Ltd.
61 Tai Seng Avenue #02-12
Singapore 534167
Tel: (65) 6280-1330; Fax: (65) 6280-6290
inquiries@periplus.com.sg; www.periplus.com

21 20 19 18          10 9 8 7 6 5 4 3 2 1
Printed in China     1806RR

# ABOUT TUTTLE:
## "Books to Span the East and West"

Our core mission at Tuttle Publishing is to create books which bring people
together one page at a time. Tuttle was founded in 1832 in the small New
England town of Rutland, Vermont (USA). Our fundamental values remain as
strong today as they were then—to publish best-in-class books informing
the English-speaking world about the countries and peoples of Asia. The
world has become a smaller place today and Asia's economic, cultural and
political influence has expanded, yet the need for meaningful dialogue and
information about this diverse region has never been greater. Since 1948,
Tuttle has been a leader in publishing books on the cultures, arts, cuisines,
languages and literatures of Asia. Our authors and photographers have won
numerous awards and Tuttle has published thousands of books on subjects
ranging from martial arts to paper crafts. We welcome you to explore the
wealth of information available on Asia at **www.tuttlepublishing.com.**